Architecture Everywhere

Investigating the Built Environment of Your Community

Joseph A. Weber

Zephyr
Press ®
REACHING THEIR HIGHEST POTENTIAL

Tucson, Arizona

Acknowledgments

In the process of researching and writing this book, there have been a number of individuals who were extremely supportive and gave generously of their time so that I might accomplish this task. Foremost is my family—my wife Kathleen, daughter Kristin, and son Neal—who spent many hours traveling hundreds of miles so I could investigate, photograph, and tour historic homes and buildings of all types. Without their understanding and patience, this book would not have been written. I also express my gratitude to Leigh Janes for her fine drawings and to Sandi Rapp, Erin Lindsey, and June Gausepohl for their patience and extra hard work in the preparation of the manuscript. I wish also to thank the members of the Department of Art and Design at Southern Illinois University at Edwardsville for their support.

Most of all, I wish to thank my mother, who, from the time I was a young boy, impressed upon me the importance of finding one's connection between family heritage and ethnic pride, and of discovering the importance of understanding one's sense of place. It was through her interest and example that I developed a respect for my "connections" and architectural heritage.

Architecture Everywhere
Investigating the Built Environment of Your Community

Grades 5–12

© 2000 by Zephyr Press
Printed in the United States of America

ISBN 1-56976-107-8

Editor: Jaelline Jaffe
Artist: Leigh Janes
Cover design: Daniel Miedaner
Design and production: Daniel Miedaner

Zephyr Press
P.O. Box 66006
Tucson, AZ 85728-6006
http://www.zephyrpress.com

Library of Congress Cataloging-in-Publication Data

Weber, Joseph, 1942-
    Architecture everywhere : investigating the built environment of your community /
  Joseph Weber.
        p. cm.
    Includes bibliographical references.
    ISBN 1-56976-107-8
    1. Architecture—United States—Study and teaching. I. Title.

NA705 .W43 1999
720'.973—dc21   99-050191

Contents

Contents

Introduction for Teachers

Architecture is a great learning tool! This resource book uses an interdisciplinary approach to teach architecture, which enhances American history, language arts, and visual and communication arts. Most of all, students discover a sense of belonging when they learn about local buildings and the history of their community.

Following are the objectives for students:

- To gain a deeper understanding of their national, regional, and local history by studying architecture
- To examine ethnic and cultural diversity through the study of American architectural history
- To trace their own cultural heritage and genealogy
- To develop an appreciation for the humanmade environment, especially the historic buildings found in their community
- To use a time line of architectural styles to understand that our visual heritage parallels American history

In our ever-changing, fast-moving world, the permanence of our architectural roots inspires us to discover our sense of place. In the challenging and insecure time of middle and high school, a sense of place may be one of the most important needs for students to fulfill.

This book is organized to provide basic information on many aspects of American architecture. It starts by examining the students' immediate environment and continues to explore relationships between their personal humanmade world and cultural roots. They will investigate types of buildings and styles of architecture found around them, focusing especially on the development of the American home. The book concludes with a study of architects and the elements they use to create buildings. A culminating project engages students in applying their knowledge to design their own dream home.

Each unit has the following sections:

FOUNDATION

As with any building, each unit needs a solid foundation. The foundation section lists the main ideas students will learn in the unit. Next is the background information you will need to convey to students before beginning. You can either read it as is, or photocopy it for them.

DESIGN

In architecture, the design is how the architect implements the building plan. In a similar manner, the design section outlines how to implement each unit to teach the main ideas. It lists the materials you need, preparation required, and suggested guidelines.

BLUEPRINTS

The design, drawn out in detail on paper, becomes the blueprint for construction of a building. Each section's blueprints are intended to draw out students and engage them in thought and activity to further their interest and knowledge about the ideas presented. Comments and questions guide students in examining the photographs. Shaded boxes contain activities that direct them to active involvement in research or production to apply their new knowledge.

CONSTRUCTION: MORE ARCHITECTURAL ADVENTURES

In the world of architecture, after the design is translated into blueprints, the builder follows the plans to construct the building. In this book, the construction is the application and extension of the students' new knowledge. Each section within the units ends with a corresponding list of architectural adventures, activities developed to extend students' learning in a variety of ways. The activities themselves appear at the end of each unit. These architectural adventures use an exciting array of approaches and modalities to engage the varied interests and learning styles of your students.

RESOURCE SHELF

Every architect has a wide range of resources available to assist with the many details necessary to create a functional and aesthetically pleasing building. This book contains many photographs, a glossary of terms, and a bibliography for you as well as for your students. In addition, your class will need to use other resources such as the Internet, library, various local community agencies, and primary sources. Suggested resources and other supplemental information are listed below the heading "resource shelf." I have included a resource shelf wherever I thought students or you might need extra resources for the activity.

THINGS TO DO AND REMEMBER WHEN USING THIS BOOK

- Prepare by reading the introduction to each unit and section to get a feel for the topic. I have described the specific teaching aims.
- Use the photographs and drawings in the figures, and gather others for the discussions. The figures are numbered sequentially in the units. Figure 1-5 is the fifth figure in the first unit.
- Read the blueprints in the student section aloud or photocopy them for students to read individually or in small groups. Give them additional suggested materials to explore and research the topics further.

- Choose additional activities from the architectural adventures at the end of the units for students to explore themes or topics. The activities are also numbered sequentially; architectural adventure 1-5 is the fifth activity in unit 1. The adventures are designed to be photocopied easily.
- A few architectural adventures require a camcorder, audiocassette recorder, 35mm camera, or the corresponding players. However, students can easily substitute a drawing if cameras are not available.
- Consider how to structure activities for your students: you may want to assign some activities to the entire class, divide them among students, or skip those you do not feel are useful or appropriate for your class or community.
- You'll present some activities to the class, but students will do them individually. Students will complete others in small groups.
- Architectural adventure 4-9, page 107, requires students to develop an architectural firm that students will work with to complete other activities. By the time you get to that activity, you should have a good idea of your students' skills. Make sure that the firms include students with diverse strengths and abilities. Balance teams so they will work well together.
- Share, display, or publish student projects. This step is extremely important because sharing their work helps students understand the topics even more deeply. The classroom, media center, local library, and city hall are all places that might display student work.
- Mount and laminate projects you wish to keep for future classes.

ICONS USED IN THE ARCHITECTURAL ADVENTURES

 Model

 Research

 Research or Design by Computer/Internet

 Audiotape

 Videotape

 Written Report

 Photographs

 Interviews

 Drawings

Introduction for Students

We are deeply rooted in culture, places, and people.
Architecture is part of a continuity.
—Charles Moore

Think of the important things you have experienced in your life. You have memories of some interesting and wonderful events. Perhaps some special people come to mind, as well as fun-filled adventures. Can you recall one day, a day that stands out above all others? Was it a special birthday, homecoming, or holiday? Was it a day when you accomplished something grand? Did a special person or pet come into your life that day? Did you win a competition, championship, game, or prize? Where did those special memories occur?

No matter where the special events or experiences occurred, we can usually associate memories with buildings. Whether they are in the country, city, faraway land, or small town, buildings play a big role in our memory of some fond or special events.

This series of units will show you how we can learn many things about ourselves and other subjects through the study of buildings. *Architecture* means the design of buildings. By studying architecture, we learn about our cultural roots, the history of our local community, and our humanmade environment. We will learn that American architecture has a unique appearance called *style* and a distinguished time line that corresponds to styles. We will study how the home was and still is prized by American families. We will examine how architects work and apply design elements in the process of creating buildings. We'll have the opportunity to draw and construct many fascinating structures, including our own dream home. But most of all, by studying American architecture, we will learn about ourselves and our connection to the past and our humanmade world, our sense of place.

Unit 1

What Is a Sense of Place?

Do I Have One?

We shape our buildings and then our buildings shape us.
—Sir Winston Churchill

FOUNDATION

IN THIS UNIT, STUDENTS DISCOVER

- BUILDINGS AND OTHER STRUCTURES HAVE BEEN BUILT TO SERVE HUMAN NEEDS.

- HOMES AND NEIGHBORHOODS REVEAL MUCH ABOUT THE PEOPLE WHO LIVE AND WORK THERE.

- MOST OF OUR MEMORIES ARE CONNECTED WITH OUR HOMES AND OTHER BUILDINGS.

- VISUAL ARTISTS OFTEN INFUSE THEIR ARTWORK WITH THE PERSONAL EXPERIENCES THEY HAVE HAD WITH HUMANMADE STRUCTURES.

Photocopy the following and pass it out to students, read it aloud to them, or use your own way of getting the concepts across to them:

We human beings encounter our environment all day long. In this encounter, we use our senses to touch, hear, smell, taste, and see the world around us. This environment is either natural, such as trees, plants, animals, and water, or it is humanmade. The humanmade environment consists of structures built to serve the needs and functions of humans. Such structures include buildings, parks, monuments, infrastructures, or support systems such as highways and bridges. Buildings are all around us and have been built to serve our various functions. Some of these buildings are houses, apartments, schools, churches, factories, and gas stations. There are many different types of these buildings, and they change in appearance and design, reflecting the time they were built and the needs of the people who used them. The interior and exterior space of each building or other humanmade structure is unique to the needs of the people who live and work in it. It serves some function of its occupants and, consequently, takes on a special form or appearance.

Exploring our humanmade environment is important for several reasons. It helps us to discover things about ourselves we didn't know or have forgotten. We can recover our first impressions, feelings about a place, and memories of things that happened in that place. Such discoveries are important because they assist us in understanding ourselves and where we fit into our past. We learn about our identity, things that make each of us special and interesting. Discovering feelings and memories from the past helps us understand that we are unique. Our surroundings, our humanmade environment, contribute to our uniqueness.

LOOKING AT OUR HUMANMADE WORLD

DESIGN

MAIN IDEAS IN THIS SECTION

- Humanmade structures are all around us, and we interact with them all day long in many different ways.
- Humanmade structures are designed to serve various functions and are made from various materials so they have unique appearances.
- When we interact with buildings, we remember special associations with them.

MATERIALS

▶ figures 1-1 through 1-4 (see pages 28–29 for enlarged photos)

FIGURE 1-1

FIGURE 1-2

FIGURE 1-3

FIGURE 1-4

OPTIONAL MATERIALS

▶ photographs of buildings in your community that parallel those in the figures
▶ photographs from newspapers or historical societies

GUIDELINES FOR INSTRUCTION

After reading the blueprints section, allow time for students to reflect and share their ideas. Discuss with students the humanmade environment that surrounds your school. In a class brainstorming activity, list the varieties of humanmade structures and their uses.

BLUEPRINTS
LOOKING AT OUR HUMANMADE WORLD

Photocopy the following section for students to read or read it aloud to them.

Examine the photographs (figures 1-1 through 1-4) and consider where each building is located. Is it in a city, a small town, a rural area? What types of activities take place in each? What kinds of occupations do the people who work there have? What materials were used to build the structures? How can you tell if the buildings are new or old? What determines how a building is designed? In what ways is a bank building different from a fast-food building?

> List all the activities you do during the week and on the weekend. Then write down the building in which each activity takes place and put an asterisk by any buildings that have special significance for you.

CONSTRUCTION
MORE ARCHITECTURAL ADVENTURES

HOMES AND NEIGHBORHOODS— A MIX FOR REMEMBERING

DESIGN

MAIN IDEAS IN THIS SECTION

- Our homes and neighborhoods are the place for discovering a connection between the outside world and ourselves.
- Each home and neighborhood we grow up in is special because it has unique features, characteristics, functions, and appearance.
- Each home or structure in a neighborhood provides for the needs and lifestyles of the people who live and work there.
- Through our neighborhood experiences, we learn about special and unique characteristics we, our relatives, and friends have.

MATERIALS

▶ figures 1-5 through 1-8 (see pages 30–31 for enlarged photos)

FIGURE 1-5

FIGURE 1-6

FIGURE 1-7

FIGURE 1-8

OPTIONAL MATERIALS

▶ other photographs of homes and families
▶ students' photographs of homes and families

GUIDELINES FOR INSTRUCTION

Read the visualization in the blueprints section to your students. Guide them through the questions. Suggest they close or cover their eyes so they can see the images in their minds' eyes. As each idea is presented, pause to allow time for images to arise. After reading, discuss the spaces they discovered and created in their own homes and neighborhoods.

BLUEPRINTS
HOMES AND NEIGHBORHOODS— A MIX FOR REMEMBERING

VISUALIZATION

Your first interactions with your humanmade environment probably were in your home. As an infant you looked around your home and experienced moving shapes, patterns of light, and sounds of people, as well as sounds of appliances, cars, and family pets. Many of these experiences were from your baby bed, car seat, or someone's arms.

As you grew older, you increased your experiences of the human-made environment by actively interacting with the space inside this environment. You no doubt crawled across the floor. The floor surface was either hard, such as tile, wood, or concrete, or soft, such as carpeting or area rugs. The feel of the floor beneath your tiny fingers was soft, thick, or even bumpy.

From crawling around your home, you gradually pulled yourself up on various pieces of furniture, walls, and stair rails, readying your-self to walk. Stairs were always interesting and especially inviting to explore. You could go up or down stairs. Gradually, as you gained confidence, you explored your humanmade environment with ease by walking. Walking from room to room, interacting with the space and furniture and other objects in each room, was easy and fun.

Creating new space from existing areas is an exciting way to change the environment. You wanted to create your own space to explore. You may have played under the dining room or kitchen table, or created your very own special playhouse under the stairs or between beds or couches. These activities were your first attempts at creating your own humanmade environment—creating a space to fit your own needs.

As you got older you experienced more spaces, more humanmade environments. You discovered the outside space of your house or apartment and its appearance. You also enjoyed experiencing the humanmade structures of the people in your life or in your neighborhood.

Architecture Everywhere, © 2000 Zephyr Press, Tucson, Arizona

Neighborhoods often reflect the culture of the people who live there. The food they prepare, the festivals they celebrate, the languages they speak, the religious ceremonies they attend, the customs they have, all are played out like a drama or play in the neighborhood. As you grew, you may have experienced such activities in your neighborhood.

Some neighborhoods in the city are combinations of retail businesses on the lower level and residential or living quarters on the top story. Some neighborhoods have houses that look almost identical to one another. Other neighborhoods are all high-rise apartments where rooftop pools, tennis courts, handball courts, and play equipment are the only yards for playing. Sometimes the balconies of each apartment are the only place for a vest-pocket yard. Your own home, play areas, and neighborhood are special because they are where you grow up and learn many things.

Photocopy the following and pass it out to students, read it aloud to them, or use your own way of getting the concepts across to them:

Study the photographs (figures 1-5 through 1-8) and think about your neighborhood. Does it have houses, apartment buildings, churches, stores, schools, or parks? Is it out in the country? Bring to mind the sights, sounds, and smells. Sense the feel of the color and shapes of the houses, places of worship, and stores. In what ways is your neighbor's home different from your own? In what ways does your grandparents' home differ in size and appearance from yours? Your friend's home and especially his or her room and the special places in which you enjoy playing are probably important to you. Is your favorite play environment a tree house, a porch, a garage, or someplace else? Does your neighborhood reflect a particular culture? Where are the houses, businesses, and other buildings located?

Humans need to find comfort and security in their neighborhoods. Take a mental inventory of everything in your neighborhood and make a list. Write several paragraphs, take photographs, or make sketches of your neighborhood. Compare and contrast these with what other students discover in their neighborhoods.

CONSTRUCTION
MORE ARCHITECTURAL ADVENTURES

Architecture Everywhere, © 2000 Zephyr Press, Tucson, Arizona

SPECIAL PEOPLE— MEMORIES AND A SENSE OF PLACE

DESIGN

MAIN IDEAS IN THIS SECTION

- We all have memories connected to the place we call home.
- In our homes, we experience events that are special to us.
- Expressing these various events permits us to become reacquainted with our homes and neighborhoods.
- Using our senses to see, smell, hear, taste, and touch our environments helps us to heighten our awareness of special memories that occurred in our homes.

MATERIALS

▶ figures 1-9 through 1-11 (see page 32 for enlarged photos)

FIGURE 1-9

FIGURE 1-10

FIGURE 1-11

OPTIONAL MATERIALS

▶ Students' photographs of family events, especially those that take place in homes or other buildings

GUIDELINES FOR INSTRUCTION

Read the visualization in the blueprints section that guides students through a mental tour of their homes and the events that take place there. You might post or circulate figures 1-9 through 1-11 beforehand, and then ask students to close or cover their eyes while you read to them, or pause during the reading so they can look at each photograph as you describe it.

Discuss with students some of their positive and negative memories of their homes. Ask them to think of the buildings or other built spaces that contributed to the moods associated with the events.

CAUTION: While many of your students may have generally happy memories associated with their homes, others may not. They may have moved many times, had unpleasant life experiences, or had significant people leave their home under unhappy circumstances. Be aware of these possibilities and be sensitive in your wording of activities so that all students can participate comfortably.

<u>BLUEPRINTS</u>
SPECIAL PEOPLE—
MEMORIES AND A SENSE OF PLACE

VISUALIZATION

When we spend time thinking about past events, no doubt we are thinking about the people associated with those events, the feelings they and we had at that time, perhaps the joy and excitement, the mood we all were in. Perhaps the event set a mood that was further created by our surroundings at the time. An example could be a party. There may have been music and special foods or decorations to enhance the mood of the party. Often the special room we were in or the buildings in which we interacted all contributed to the festive feeling or mood of that time. When we think about such things or daydream about them, we are using memory. Memories are thoughts left from our experiences. Do you remember ever being in a place like that in figure 1-9?

Memories help to tell us about ourselves and what unique things happened to us as human beings. Of course, not all memories are pleasant, joyful, or good. We all have those memories we would like to forget, but those, too, are part of our life experiences.

Often buildings and architecture bring to mind memories that cause us to think about ourselves and our environment. They also cause us to think about our culture now and in the past. Thinking of memories related to specific buildings in our lives will help us rediscover things about ourselves. These memories are a visual scrapbook of our lives. They help us to get in touch with ourselves in ways we might have forgotten. Buildings might provide the key.

Let's go on a mental tour of the place where you live. Visualize the inside of your home. Think of the events that take place there; they involve you, your family, and friends. Start with the place where you sleep. Do you have your own room, do you share it with others, or is it a community place in your home? How is your space similar to or different from the room in figure 1-10? What is special about your space? How does it reflect your personality or interests? Do you put posters or pictures and other things on the walls? Is your space a place for friends to talk or discuss homework? Do you play music or watch TV there? Do you have a computer or video games?

In the kitchen, do you help prepare special meals or create favorite recipes for your family? What pleasant aromas remind you of your home? Can you recall any funny, embarrassing, or disquieting stories about kitchen chores or family encounters in the kitchen?

Where do you eat meals? Do people in your home eat together or at different times? Do you remember any especially interesting discussions or disagreements that occurred at mealtime? Was it here that you heard some sad or happy news about family, friends, or things happening in the world?

Is there a time when everyone in your family gathers in one room to share special events such as unwrapping presents or entertaining relatives and family friends? In what room do they gather? Do you also watch TV in this room or dance or play music there?

In some parts of the country, the basement is used to store many things that are no longer needed or wanted, or have been outgrown. Surely this place, with its castoffs, brings back memories. The garage, too, may house a collection of "stuff," memories of times and neighborhood children and past or present activities. Where does your family store its stuff? Your bikes, skateboards, and baseball gear may have found a home here. Is it a place you play in on a rainy day? Attics often have a romantic association—mysterious banishment in many classic novels . . . journals . . . love letters . . . trinkets with special memories. Do you have a room or space that serves as the "attic" in your home? Do you ever play or hunt through treasures there?

Do you have a yard or other space around your house or apartment building? Is it the place where you play ball or other games, or just "hang out" with friends? Do you have picnics and barbecues there? What kinds of other activities do you do there? What chores do you have to do in that place? Do you have a secret hiding place built in some inconspicuous spot?

Look at figure 1-11. Does your home have a porch with a swing or porch furniture? If not, what area around your home serves the same function as a porch? Your memories may include sitting on the porch swing or on the stairs in the summer, experiencing cool breezes, and talking with family or friends. If you carve a jack-o-lantern on Halloween, where do you put it? How do you decorate for the holidays that your family celebrates?

Now that you have taken a mental tour of your home, select at least three areas of it, including the outside areas. Write one or more paragraphs about each area, recalling your responses to the questions raised in your mental tour. Include the special people who are a part of your memories. Share your writing with a partner in your class, one whose home you have never visited. As you listen to your partner, visualize what his or her home looks like, and get a sense of how he or she experiences it.

CONSTRUCTION
MORE ARCHITECTURAL ADVENTURES

Architecture Everywhere, © 2000 Zephyr Press, Tucson, Arizona

How Visual Artists Share Experiences and Memories

Design

Main Ideas in This Section

- Visual artists often use humanmade structures in their work.
- The artist communicates an experience with a humanmade structure through the use of mood, color, texture, time of day or season, and with the medium.
- America is rich with a wide variety of visual artists who have used the humanmade environment as a source of inspiration over the centuries and who continue to do so today.
- We can develop some skills in analyzing visual works of art in the context of the artist's intentions.
- We can determine the meaning of works of art and our aesthetic preferences.

Materials

▶ figures 1-12 through 1-13 (see pages 33–34 for enlarged photos)

FIGURE 1-12

FIGURE 1-13

Guidelines for Instruction

Ask students to read the description of the two artists in the blueprint section. Discuss with students the idea that visual artists—writers, composers, photographers, and cinematographers—draw from experience for their art. Often their experiences with buildings become the major focus of their work. Guide students through the comparison of the work of two American artists. Ask them to research other artists who use the humanmade environment in their work.

BLUEPRINTS
HOW ARTISTS SHARE EXPERIENCES AND MEMORIES

Photocopy the following and pass it out to students, read it aloud to them, or use your own way of getting the concepts across to them:

Over the years, American artists have used their houses, neighborhoods, or other aspects of the humanmade environment as sources of inspiration. Like you, they have memories of some special activity and person-to-person interaction within the humanmade environment. They use this account of what they felt about their special spaces, the people in the spaces, the time of day or season in their work. Some find interest and beauty in the place where they grew up and have fond memories of that place, which then served as inspiration for their artwork. This inspiration is expressed in paintings, photographs, drawings, prints, sculpture, and ceramics. In these ways, artists try to capture the feelings and moods they associate with the memories of a special place. Some artists share special traditions that were part of their heritage. These traditions were centered around certain humanmade places. Architectural landmarks can also be sources of inspiration.

Before selecting artists to research, read the following passage to help you compare and contrast two works of art by well-known American artists from different times who use the humanmade environment as their source of inspiration:

> **Charles Sheeler** (1883–1965), a painter and photographer, was born in Philadelphia, Pennsylvania, and studied at the Philadelphia School of Industrial Art and Pennsylvania Academy of Fine Art. His work was included in the Armory Show of 1913. In the 1920s, his paintings emphasized Early American handicrafts, especially of the Shakers, and the folk architecture of Doylestown, Pennsylvania, where he lived. He used such architectural forms and elements to express a sense of order, portraying specifically sharp edges and clearly defined planes. He turned from this subject matter to painting large cities and old factories, abstracting their shapes and using bright colors. He painted *Home Sweet Home* (figure 1-12) in 1931. It is oil on canvas, 36 inches by 29 inches.

Richard Estes (1936–), born in Kewane, Illinois, was trained as an illustrator and later turned to fine art. His style of painting is associated with the hyper-realist movement. The goal of the hyper-realists is to paint the humanmade world in a photographic, realistic manner, usually in large format. Estes's paintings are based on his own photographs of the humanmade environment. His subject matter is the urban landscape, particularly New York City, where he lives. He re-creates this landscape with painstaking detail. He likes the effects of light on objects, reflections and refraction, transparency and opacity on a variety of surfaces. *Helene's Florist* (figure 1-13), painted in 1971, is a good example of his style. It is oil on canvas, 48 inches by 72 inches.

Use the following process to critique each work of art so you can decide if you like or dislike it.

Step 1. List everything you see in each painting. Include objects, shapes, colors, textures, patterns, and so on. Compare the elements of the two paintings.

Step 2. Identify the elements or principles of design—shape, texture, contrast, movement, color, space, balance, rhythm, center of interest, perspective, depth—that the artists use to create or organize the compositions. Consider also painting techniques such as clarity of edges and the mood communicated through the technique.

Step 3. Relate what the artists are saying about the subject. What statements or ideas do you think they are sharing with us about their humanmade world? What medium or process is each artist using to make this statement? What do you think is the meaning or purpose of each painting?

Step 4. After comparing the two works, decide which painting you like best. State your reasons based on steps 1, 2, and 3.

Continue to research the work and lives of Charles Sheeler and Richard Estes. Discover more about the influences of the humanmade environment on the artists. How do their other works compare with those included here?

Architecture Everywhere, © 2000 Zephyr Press, Tucson, Arizona

15

To analyze how American artists use their humanmade environment as inspiration for their artwork, investigate a wide variety of artists from different time periods. Use the library or Internet to identify American artists who use the humanmade environment in their paintings, photographs, drawings, sculpture, or ceramics. Select an artist whose work appeals to you and research that artist in more depth. Include the artist's general background and the time in which he or she lived or lives. Select a work and write a description of the elements that convey the artist's connection to the humanmade place depicted. Concentrate on mood, color, types of structures, time of year, and use of light. Then use the four steps to analyze how the humanmade environment was used in the work. Make a class presentation to show your progress toward becoming an art critic.

RESOURCE SHELF

- ▶ library
- ▶ museum collections on the Internet
- ▶ local art museums or galleries
- ▶ local poster or picture shop

CONSTRUCTION
MORE ARCHITECTURAL ADVENTURES

1-18: Investigating American Painters, Sculptors, and Illustrators (page 26)

1-19: My Favorite Object Captured and Enlarged (page 26)

MORE ARCHITECTURAL ADVENTURES

1-1: THIS IS WHERE I LIVE

Expand on the mental tour of your home. Write a description of, draw, create a scrapbook of, or write a song about your home or your space. If you have lived in more than one home or have had several different rooms, pick the one that you most cherish. In describing your home and room, include the following:

- ▶ your favorite toys, games, and other items
- ▶ special events or celebrations
- ▶ upsetting or disappointing days that occurred there
- ▶ your favorite places in the home and reasons
- ▶ your most cherished memory about the home

1-2: CREATING A VIDEOTAPE ABOUT MY COMMUNITY

Create a videotape that shows the history of your community. If you live in a large metropolitan area, divide the city into segments and assign them to small groups in your class. First, look at the time line from the last activity and decide where and what you will need to record. Perhaps someone can be the moderator or person on the street who describes the events or places that were important to understanding these special places. Include the following:

- ▶ place of the earliest settlement and any remaining structures
- ▶ significant events, when and where they occurred
- ▶ various types of commercial, retail, and residential buildings that were typical in each era you have included on your time line
- ▶ monuments, markers, or other sites (war monuments, cannons, memorials) that honor specific events or people in your community's history

Supplement your video with posters, newspaper headlines, pictures, and music that contribute to a well-rounded presentation to the class or the school.

1-3: A PHOTOGRAPH AND DRAWING ESSAY OF WHERE I LIVE

Create a photograph or drawing essay of your humanmade environment. With a camera, drawing pencils, or markers, photograph or sketch buildings, monuments, and recreational sites that are very important to you. Consider places such as your room or other space, home, neighborhood, grandparents' home, school, place of worship, stores, restaurants, play areas. Include as many photographs and drawings as possible so you can present them to your classmates. Mat or frame your photographs and drawings, and arrange them in a meaningful sequence. Hang them in the classroom for all to see.

1-4: IT'S ABOUT TIME: A TIME LINE ABOUT OUR COMMUNITY

A time line of your community provides you and your classmates with a point of reference for the history of your city. Depending on the age of your community, you can do this activity individually or with partners or teams each taking a particular time. First gather information about the significant events in the history of your community. As a class, decide what colors will represent what types of events (for example, yellow for happy celebrations, blue for tragedies, green for changes or growth). Using either colored index cards or colored markers on white cards, transfer the information you have gathered about each event onto the appropriately colored card. Include dates, facts, and pictures. Hang them in sequence on a clothesline in the classroom.

RESOURCE SHELF

- ▶ local library or newspaper archives
- ▶ state or county historical societies
- ▶ county courthouse, especially departments for plans and records, and for recording of deeds
- ▶ local historical committees or commissions
- ▶ genealogy societies
- ▶ history teachers
- ▶ historical organizations such as the Daughters of the American Revolution, Sons and Daughters of the Union, Sons and Daughters of the Confederacy
- ▶ ethnic fraternal organizations

Architecture Everywhere, © 2000 Zephyr Press, Tucson, Arizona

1-5: MY ABODE, MY NEIGHBORHOOD

The neighborhood where we grow up is special. It is where we meet other kids in the area and play, walk to school or catch the bus, have gatherings or parties, and interact with our neighbors.

Write an essay about your neighborhood. Include the types of buildings you encounter: houses, apartments, stores, churches, schools. Describe the appearance of these structures. Write about the people who live in your neighborhood and the special associations and memories that you have of them. Did you used to play at a particular friend's home? Did you have a secret language? Where do you hang out with your neighborhood friends now? Have you created secret places to meet? Did you have a clubhouse or other special gathering place?

Use colored pencils or thin-tipped markers to draw your home and neighborhood. Show in your drawings the various building materials used in structures. You may want to look ahead to the one- and two-point perspective activity on page 25. Exhibit your drawings in the classroom.

1-6: A PHOTOMONTAGE OF MY FAVORITE PLACE

A photomontage is a collage of photographs that are cut or torn out and arranged on a flat surface. This activity is like writing an essay, but instead of using words, you use images to illustrate various thoughts or perspectives. Take a series of photographs of many different views of buildings, objects, and people who are or were part of your neighborhood. You may also use magazines or old photographs in your montage. Cut or tear away unnecessary parts. Arrange the pictures and glue them on a piece of mat or foam board. Frame your photomontage. Display it for your classmates, and discuss the significance of the images you incorporated.

1-7: CREATING A TIME CAPSULE

A time capsule is a container that is usually put into a cornerstone of a building when the building is being erected. The date of construction is engraved on the cornerstone. Inside the capsule are pictures, newspaper articles, mementos, and artifacts that are popular and culturally significant at the time of construction. At some set future date, people pull out the time capsule to study and reflect on the time the building was erected. The time capsule allows us to save the past and reflect on the important or significant facts of that time.

Brainstorm with the class a list of several types of buildings (school, library, hospital, police station, office, government). Copy each onto a separate slip of paper. Place the slips into a container and pull one out.

You will create your own time capsule for the cornerstone of the building on the slip. Make or find a container to serve as your time capsule. Perhaps your container can reflect the specific type of building in which it will be placed. Put into the capsule things that you feel reflect this time as well as the purposes of your particular building. Think about what might be of interest to someone of your current age seventy years from now—perhaps your great-grandchild.

Now imagine it is seventy or more years in the future. Have a celebration in your classroom and display all the capsules. Each student will play the part of a person who knows little of the past and will open a capsule that was created by someone else, show the class the contents, and explain what each item is and why it may have been included in the cornerstone of that building.

1-8: CONVERSATIONS WITH SPECIAL RELATIVES

Oral histories—especially those shared by your parents, grandparents, aunts, or uncles—can be a worthwhile part of helping you understand your family and its history. Remembrances of your relatives from times and events long ago are special. Interview relatives or ask them to share such events. Capture these thoughts on audio- or videotape so you have a record of these special people and their views to cherish forever. Following are some suggested topics about which to ask them:

- ▶ place they were born and how they came to America
- ▶ place they entered the country, or places they have lived
- ▶ their homes and other buildings that were important to them as children
- ▶ their lives as children, including meals, and indoor and outdoor chores
- ▶ their lives then compared to now, including important buildings
- ▶ school experiences, including the school building
- ▶ their dreams of what they wanted to become when they grew up
- ▶ types of work they did and wages for the work, including the buildings they worked in
- ▶ types of transportation
- ▶ types of heating and cooling in their homes
- ▶ sports or other recreational activities they took part in and the places they did them
- ▶ world fairs, expositions, or local fairs, and the places in which they were held

Architecture Everywhere, © 2000 Zephyr Press, Tucson, Arizona

▶ holidays and festivals and the places they celebrated them

▶ wartime experiences

▶ ways they met their spouses

▶ their most important accomplishments or sources of pride

▶ advice they would give to you as you grow up

After taping, share the information with other family members. Date and store the tapes in a safe place for you and perhaps your own children to enjoy and treasure.

1-9: CREATING A FAMILY FACT SHEET

Use the Family Group Information Inventory in the appendix (page 196) to record information on your family and your ancestors' families. You will need to make one copy for each couple that you include. Fill in all the information you can gather, starting with your parents: their dates of birth, marriage, and death if they are no longer living. Include occupations, religious affiliations, dates of any military service, other marriages, and the names of their parents (your grandparents). Note the sources of all information. At the bottom of the chart, fill in the names of all children in the family, and the other information for each of them, including yourself. Then use additional charts for your grandparents, great-grandparents, and great- great-grandparents, if possible. You can also create charts for your aunts and uncles and their families, if you choose. If you do not have information about your biological family, you may choose to use the family you most closely identify as your own. If there have been remarriages in your family, you may choose to add extra spaces for the members they brought in.

1-10: CONSTRUCTING MY ANCESTRAL CHART

An ancestral chart shows all your parents and grandparents without any other members of their families. Use the Five-Generation Family Chart in the appendix (page 197). There may have been divorces, remarriages, or nonmarriages in your family line. You may choose to track your biological or stepparent's family line. Start by writing your name on line 1, your mother's name on line 2, and your father's name on line 3. Under each name, write in the date and place of birth, marriage, and death if the person is no longer living. Continue in the same manner with your mother's parents and your father's parents, and go back as many generations as you can. This activity may take some time to complete, so be patient. Remember: this is your activity and you may select whichever part of your family line you wish to research.

1-11: SIMULATED INTERVIEWS

By now you have found out much about your family's history and their immigration to this country. Some students' ancestors may have been here before Columbus arrived. Some students' families may have come recently. Others may have come around the beginning of the twentieth century. Still others may have come hundreds of years ago. Some may have been brought as slaves, while others may have entered the country illegally.

Imagine that you are a member of your family who was among the first to come to this country and that you want to acquire legal status. You are going to do a simulation—an imitation or modeling of the Immigration and Naturalization Service (INS) interview.

First, prepare a list of questions an immigration official might ask. Following are some possibilities:

- What is your surname (last name)?
- When and where were you born?
- When did you first leave your native country? Where did you go from there? Where else did you live before coming to America?
- Are you married? Do you have any children? Are any other family members traveling with you? Do you have any family already living in this country? Where?
- What kind of work are you trained to do?

Rearrange the classroom by moving desks or tables to form rows. Half of the class will sit behind tables and play the part of INS agents; the other half will enter the room one at a time and be directed to an agent. When you are in the role of an agent, ask your prepared list of questions and record the immigrant's answers. As the immigrant, use all the information you have gathered about your ancestors, or make some likely and intelligent guesses if you don't know the actual answers. When the interviews are complete, switch roles.

If your family heritage is Native American or enslaved American, alter the activity. Play the parts of agents of the Bureau of Indian Affairs and of your early family members who were being moved from their land to a reservation. If your ancestors were brought here as slaves, play the parts of those who were captured and the slave owners. Be sensitive to the feelings of your relatives, and attempt to understand and empathize with your classmates and their family histories.

As a class, share the experience of being the various people. Discuss the feelings that went with each role, and speculate as to how your actual ancestors might have felt in their situations.

1-12: AN AUDIOTAPE ABOUT ME

The aim of this activity is to get information about you! This exercise in oral history will provide you with ways of gathering information about you and your family. You will need a tape recorder and a notepad with questions that you may want to ask your parents, guardians, or others who knew you from your birth. Here are some suggested topics for starters:

- Where was I born?
- How did Mom get to the hospital, or was I born someplace other than a hospital?
- What buildings were around when I was born that aren't around anymore?
- Who was president when I was born?
- What were some significant news events?
- Are there any interesting stories about the day I was born?
- Where did I sleep as a baby?
- What did I do as a toddler?
- What were my favorite toys?
- Did I ever embarrass my parents in public?
- When and where did I learn to walk?
- Who else looked after me?
- What was my preschool or kindergarten building like? How did I react to my first day at preschool or kindergarten?
- What other important events do you remember about me? What buildings do you associate with those events?

1-13: WHAT A GOOD-LOOKING FAMILY!

Collect as many photographs as you can that show pictures of your family at various times in your life. Include pictures of grandparents, aunts, uncles, and cousins. Include pictures that show your home or others' homes. If your family will allow you to keep these pictures, draw or paint a large tree and arrange the pictures with related parts of the family on the branches. Now you have a variation of a visual family tree! Compare your family tree with those of your classmates, and create a class graph that shows the number of children in immediate families, as well as the number of aunts, uncles, grandparents, cousins, and so on.

1-14: NOTES ABOUT MY FAVORITE PLACE

Where is your favorite place? Is it in your home—living room, family room, basement, bedroom? Perhaps it is outside—deck, patio, or garage. Or is your favorite place other than in your home—at a friend's, local gym, video arcade? Write down all the things you associate with that place: special events, celebrations, exciting times, quiet times, comforting times, funny times, scary times. Include details, moods, colors, sounds, aromas, and items such as furniture that you connect with this special place.

1-15: CREATING A ROOMRHYME

A roomrhyme is a poem that uses words that rhyme to describe characteristics of your favorite room. Usually the roomrhyme is eight to ten lines long and tells how this room is special to you. After you have completed the roomrhyme, draw a picture or take a photograph of your special place. Display them side by side. Read your roomrhymes to others in your class and show them the photograph. Notice whether your classmates included humor, description, sentimentality, or other qualities in their roomrhymes.

1-16: DRAWING A FLOOR PLAN OF MY SPACE

Many of us have a very special, happy place we call our own. It may be our room at home or a special place in another part of our home, yard, or outside. Wherever it is, it is a place to retreat to, a place in which we spend many hours.

Draw a floor plan of your special space. Using appropriate tools, measure the length and width of the space and draw it on the graph provided in the appendix (page 198). The scale used in the graph is 1/4 inch equals 1 foot. If your space is 12 feet long, you would count twelve squares on the graph. Your 12-foot-long space would be 3 inches long on the graph.

After you have marked the length and width of the space, measure each piece of furniture: bed, dresser, closet, bookcase, desk, chairs—whatever you have. Cut the items out of the sheet in the appendix (page 199) and paste them down in your floor plan. Add any other items that you have in your space that make it yours.

1-17: DRAWING BUILDINGS OR INTERIORS IN PERSPECTIVE

There are two methods of perspective that will help you draw buildings or interiors realistically: one- and two-point perspective. Refer to the drawings in the appendix (pages 200–201) and use them as guides.

ONE-POINT PERSPECTIVE

Imagine you are in a car traveling down a street with tall skyscrapers on each side. Ahead of you is the horizon, which separates the sky from the ground. As you look forward, your eye travels to a point on the horizon straight ahead of you. The doors, windows, streets, and curbs all seem to travel to that same point. Drawing from one-point perspective makes buildings appear as if they were disappearing at that one point on the horizon. The same is true in a smaller space, such as a room in a house, only the vanishing point may be somewhere outside the walls. See the drawing in the appendix (page 200) for an example of interior one-point perspective.

To draw from one-point perspective, follow this process:

Step 1. Select a location in or around your school or home where there is at least one building and where you can see the horizon. Use a soft pencil to draw a line for the horizon on a sketch pad or on a sheet of paper.

Step 2. Choose one spot on the horizon to serve as your vanishing point. Make a dot on your line to serve as that vanishing point.

Step 3. Place a ruler so that one side rests against the vanishing point. Sketch in guide lines to serve for parts of the buildings (top and bottom, windows, doors), with all the lines intersecting the vanishing point. A ruler will help you make straight lines. Remember, you can always erase the lines you don't need and go over the dominant lines.

Step 4. Add details until the picture resembles the buildings you are drawing. For help, refer to the drawings in the appendix.

TWO-POINT PERSPECTIVE

In two-point perspective, you have two vanishing points on the horizon, which allows you to draw the corners and sides of buildings accurately.

To draw from two-point perspective, follow these steps:

Step 1. Select a building to draw, and position yourself so that one corner of the structure is closest to you and faces you. From this vantage point, you should be able to see the front or back and one side of the building.

Step 2. Choose two vanishing points on the horizon. They will be to each side of the building, and might even be so far to the side that they are off the picture plane.

Step 3. Draw a line to represent the horizon, then draw a vertical line that stops on the horizon line. The vertical line is the corner of the building. Look closely at the building you are drawing; the horizontal lines that make up the top and bottom on the front and side seem to recede. If you continued drawing them past the confines of the building, they would vanish at the two spots you have drawn on your pad. These lines are your visual guides.

Step 4. Fit in the rest of the building—windows, roofs, doors—using the guide lines. For help, refer to the drawing illustrating two-point perspective in the appendix (page 201).

You will need to practice using one- and two-point perspective. The more you practice, the more you will train your eye to draw buildings accurately. Keep a sketch book handy.

1-18: INVESTIGATING AMERICAN PAINTERS, SCULPTORS, AND ILLUSTRATORS

Read some books on American artists or find examples of their work on the Internet. Look for artists who were or are influenced by the American humanmade environment. Select one artist who attempts to portray the American scene in a way that has particular appeal to you. There are many famous visual artists, so everyone in the class should be able to choose a different one.

Research your artist. Prepare a report on this artist. Include reproductions or slides of his or her work, with several examples to portray a well-rounded picture. Analyze this artist's work in terms of the time the work was created. Now, execute your own work of art in the style and medium used by this artist. Present your report to the class and describe what you learned by re-creating a work in your artist's style.

1-19: MY FAVORITE OBJECT CAPTURED AND ENLARGED

Take a walk through your home. Select one object that you can hold in your hands, something that holds some special importance or memory, something that you cherish. With a drawing pencil, colored drawing pencils, or colored pastels, capture this object on 12-by-18-inch drawing paper. Enlarge the object, making it bigger than it really is. In the background or around this enlarged object, sketch events or people that remind you of the object and its importance to you. The background figures can blend into one another. Display your artwork in class and explain its significance.

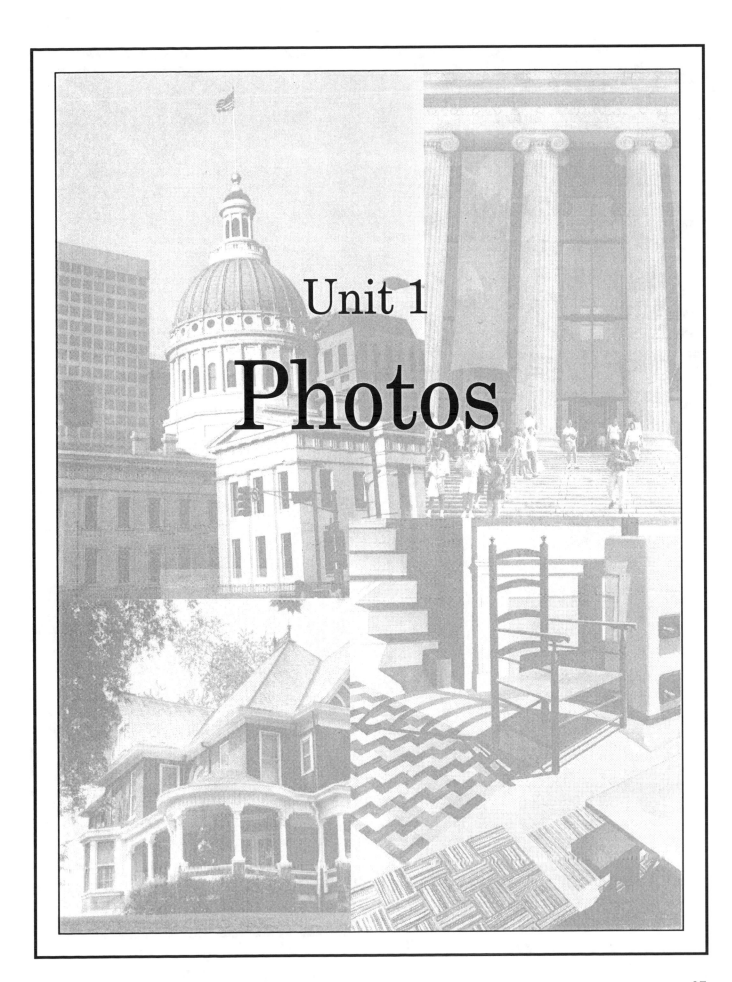

Unit 1
Photos

▶ FIGURE 1-2. AS A CLASS, WE SOMETIMES GO ON FIELD TRIPS. DID YOU EVER VISIT A MUSEUM? WHAT OTHER BUILDINGS HAVE YOU BEEN TO?

Architecture Everywhere, © 2000 Zephyr Press, Tucson, Arizona

▲ FIGURE 1-3. WHAT PURPOSE DO YOU THINK THIS BUILDING SERVES? WHAT
OUTSIDE FEATURES GIVE YOU CLUES?

▲ FIGURE 1-4. HAVE YOU BEEN TO A BASEBALL STADIUM OR ANY OTHER
TYPE OF VENUE WHERE LOTS OF PEOPLE WATCH AN EVENT AT THE SAME
TIME? RECALL THE SOUNDS, SMELLS, COLORS, MOVEMENT, AND LIGHTS
OF THE EVENT.

▲ *Figure 1-5.* Neighborhoods are important to us as we grow up. On streets such as this we meet our friends and neighbors. We explore their houses and yards, and play our games.

▲ *Figure 1-6.* We often walk from home to school or from home to the bus stop. Do you pass any houses like this one? How can you tell if this is a house or a condominium?

▲ *FIGURE 1-7. DO YOU LIKE GOING TO YOUR LOCAL PUBLIC LIBRARY? DO YOU STUDY THERE? WHAT OTHER PUBLIC BUILDINGS DO YOU USE?*

▲ *FIGURE 1-8. OLDER NEIGHBORHOODS OFTEN HAVE DISTINCTIVE ARCHITECTURAL APPEARANCES. WHAT BUILDING MATERIALS WERE USED HERE? WHY ARE THE BUILDINGS SO CLOSE TOGETHER?*

◀ **FIGURE 1-9.** WHAT BUILDINGS AND PLACES BRING BACK SPECIAL MEMORIES FOR YOU?

▶ **FIGURE 1-10.** WHAT SPECIAL THINGS DO YOU LIKE ABOUT YOUR SPACE? WHAT CHANGES WOULD YOU MAKE IF YOU COULD?

◀ **FIGURE 1-11.** DO THE HOUSES IN YOUR NEIGHBORHOOD HAVE PORCHES, STEPS, OR FRONT YARDS? DO YOU EVER PLAY ON A BIG FRONT PORCH OR SIT ON A SWING WHILE WATCHING NEIGHBORS GO BY? WHAT SOUNDS DO YOU HEAR WHEN YOU SIT OUTSIDE YOUR HOME?

Architecture Everywhere, © 2000 Zephyr Press, Tucson, Arizona

▲ FIGURE 1-12. HOME, SWEET HOME, OIL ON CANVAS. PAINTED IN 1931 BY CHARLES SHEELER, AMERICAN, 1883–1965. THE DETROIT INSTITUTE OF ARTS.

▲ FIGURE 1-13. HELENE'S FLORIST, OIL ON CANVAS. PAINTED IN 1971
BY RICHARD ESTES, AMERICAN, 1936–. THE TOLEDO ART MUSEUM.

Unit 2

Our Historical and Cultural Connections to Buildings

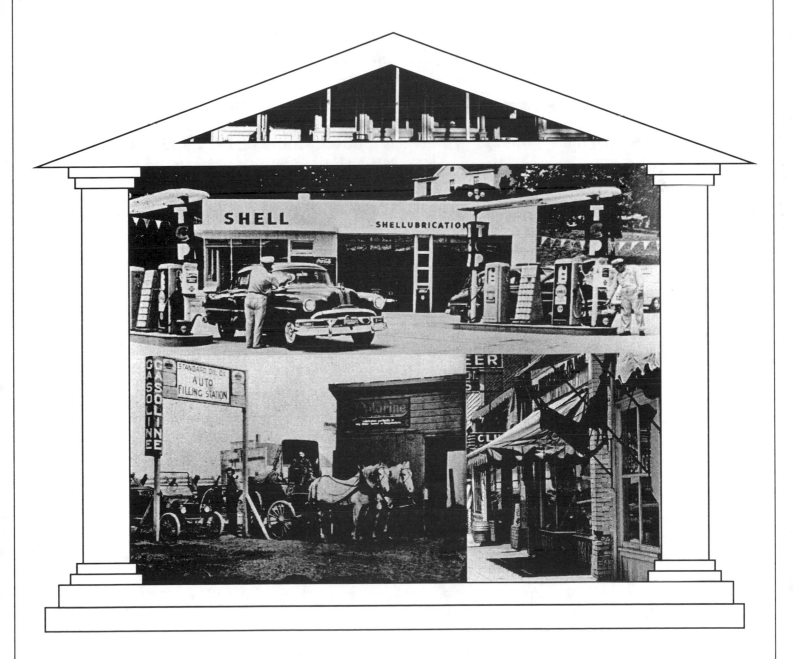

Form follows function.
—Louis Sullivan

FOUNDATION

IN THIS UNIT, STUDENTS

■ USE THEIR OWN COMMUNITY TO STUDY HOW THE HUMANMADE ENVIRONMENT HAS CHANGED.

■ USE BUILDINGS TO UNDERSTAND THEIR COMMUNITY'S HISTORY.

■ DISCOVER IF THEIR ANCESTORS LIVED AND WORKED IN THE COMMUNITY, WHICH ANCESTORS FIRST CAME TO THE REGION, AND WHY THEY CAME.

■ EXAMINE AND COMPARE WAYS ONE TYPE OF BUILDING CHANGED OVER TIME AND THE IMPACT OF NEW INVENTIONS AND TECHNOLOGIES.

Photocopy the following and pass it out to students, read it aloud to them, or use your own way of getting the concepts across to them:

We have considered ways our first experiences with the humanmade environment started in our homes and expanded into our neighborhoods. Our memories often center on special people doing things in special places. By thinking about ways that our humanmade world affects us, we begin to see how we find our sense of place in our environment. We have also researched how the humanmade environment provides inspiration for artists in their drawings, paintings, sculptures, or photographs.

Another way we can become connected to our humanmade environment and further develop our sense of place is to study the buildings in our community. Regardless of size, every community has buildings that were built at different times to serve the various needs of the community. These buildings were built with materials and construction techniques that were popular at the time and reflect a certain appearance that was thought to be practical or beautiful. When we research the various buildings in our community, we learn about its history and the people who settled here, and we understand how buildings change with the times. Our buildings serve as a visible history or time line of our community.

While it is true every community has a time line, some communities are much older than others. However, American buildings constructed at a given time or date will be similar in appearance no matter where they were built. They share a particular style. Some communities have preserved their buildings more effectively than others. Photographs or drawings may be all that is left of the oldest structures in other communities and will be found only in local libraries or historical societies either in the city or in the state capital library. In some communities, the oldest buildings may have been covered with different facades or additions to the front, side, or back.

Architecture Everywhere, © 2000 Zephyr Press, Tucson, Arizona

Buildings All around Town— A Visible Reminder of People, Ideas, and Their Time

Design

Main Ideas in This Section

- The humanmade environment found in each community is a visible reminder of various times.
- When we study the buildings in our community, we put together a time line of local history
- By studying buildings, we gain insight into the people who built them and the particular values they had at the time.
- By studying buildings, we can identify inventions and new technologies that had profound impacts on the way people lived and the ways they built structures within their times.

Materials

▶ 35 mm camera or other camera

Guidelines for Instruction

Arrange a bus or walking tour of several local points of interest (older buildings, historical societies, house museums, local and state libraries, cemeteries, the industrial areas, county courthouse). Ask them to take photographs. If you go together, ask the questions in the blueprints section as you proceed. If they go on their own, duplicate the questions for them to answer and have them report back to the class.

Resource Shelf

▶ pictures or photographs of local buildings
▶ local historians
▶ books on state history

BLUEPRINTS

BUILDINGS ALL AROUND TOWN—A VISIBLE REMINDER OF PEOPLE, IDEAS, AND THEIR TIME

Photocopy the following and pass it out to students, read it aloud to them, or use your own way of getting the concepts across to them:

We're going to take a trip around our community. Look at all of the buildings you see. Take photographs or find old photographs of the community for us to display in the classroom. Draw or sketch the buildings or specific architectural details, especially ones that appeal to you. Identify special features such as windows, doors, and roofs, and architectural details such as carvings, trims, textures, or colors. What materials were used to build the structures?

How can you determine which buildings are the oldest? Find out the dates when they were constructed. Start putting together an architectural time line with the oldest buildings first. Continue with your time line, finding examples of buildings in every era up to the present.

Choose one option below. You will find the information, then prepare the product listed to present to the class.

- Read all you can about the development of our community. Who were the settlers of the community? When and why did they come to this area? What were the main places of employment? Is the community known for its special factories or industries? If so, research the beginning of these major places of employment.

- Were your ancestors or those of any of your acquaintances among the first settlers in our community? What did they do for a living? Where did they work? Create a family album, collage, or assemblage of your family's connection to your town. In this way you and others can see your personal connection to your town and sense of belonging.

- Do you live on a farm? Is it the family farm? When was the homestead developed? How has it changed over the years? Create a display of your family's connection or life on the farm. Prepare a visual time line of how life on the farm has changed, paying special attention to its buildings. You may find it helpful to talk with older farmers for information. The local Farm Bureau may help you as well.

CONSTRUCTION
MORE ARCHITECTURAL ADVENTURES

SHOPPING AROUND

DESIGN

MAIN IDEAS IN THIS SECTION

- Goods and services are provided to the community in certain buildings designed for convenience; the buildings' appearance and design reflect the style of the time they were built.
- When additional transportation options are made available to people, the growth of the community expands outward, and consequently the major shopping areas also change location and appearance.
- Lifestyle and changing demographics contribute to where and how we shop.
- The same changes that affect people shape the way humanmade structures such as schools, churches, and banks evolve over time.

MATERIALS

▶ figures 2-1 through 2-4 (see pages 54–55 for enlarged photos)

FIGURE 2-1

FIGURE 2-2

FIGURE 2-3

FIGURE 2-4

▶ reprints of Victorian-era Sears and Roebuck catalogs for types of merchandise available then

BLUEPRINTS
SHOPPING AROUND

Photocopy the following and pass it out to students, read it aloud to them, or use your own way of getting the concepts across to them:

Do you like to shop? What do you like to buy? Many people love to explore various stores and check out the latest merchandise. This activity isn't new. For centuries people have been motivated to buy things. What has changed is where we shop, the places where the stores have been built, our shopping habits, and the appearance of stores. In studying how we shop, we understand how our communities have also changed to meet our shopping requirements.

Inspect the photographs in figures 2-1 through 2-4. What places or stores do you see? What inventions do you see? In what era were the pictures taken? What elements of the buildings make you think they were taken in that era? What type of merchandise would be purchased in each store at that time? What changes do you see in the stores? What unique architectural designs or elements can you find in each photograph? What type of material was used at what time to construct the buildings? What unique elements of the signs reflect that time? Do similar buildings still exist in your community?

Write a paragraph about each photograph; include your responses to the questions. Speculate on how shopping has changed over the years and why.

Photograph or sketch similar shopping areas in your community. Organize your photographs or sketches by age of the buildings and add them to the time line you began in the previous unit. Compare and contrast the construction techniques, signage, construction materials, design, and color of your community's buildings with those in the figures. Identify other humanmade structures in your community such as office buildings, churches, and schools that have changed over time.

CONSTRUCTION
MORE ARCHITECTURAL ADVENTURES

2-6: Tracking It Down: Changes in Types of Architecture over Time (page 49)

THE GAS STATION AND THE AUTOMOBILE CULTURE

DESIGN

MAIN IDEAS IN THIS SECTION

- The automobile and its creation had a significant impact on American life.
- The gas station evolved as an example of architecture and has changed during the past ninety years.
- Other examples of architecture and engineering are associated with our automobile culture.

MATERIALS

► figures 2-5 through 2-10 (see pages 56–57 for enlarged photos)

FIGURE 2-5

FIGURE 2-6

FIGURE 2-7

FIGURE 2-8

FIGURE 2-9

FIGURE 2-10

OPTIONAL MATERIALS

► pictures of cars from various eras
► automobile advertisements from the past and present
► information on architecture that depends on the automobile (restaurants, banks, post offices)
► information about and pictures of highways, bridges, and tunnels

Architecture Everywhere, © 2000 Zephyr Press, Tucson, Arizona

BLUEPRINTS

THE GAS STATION AND THE AUTOMOBILE CULTURE

Photocopy the following and pass it out to students, read it aloud to them, or use your own way of getting the concepts across to them:

An important goal of most of you is to get your driver's license. But did you ever consider how the automobile has changed the American landscape and our lifestyle? For example, it has had a profound impact on our cities, towns, and farms. You'll explore various forms of architecture and engineering that emerged because of the automobile. The gas station was the first such form to appear on the scene. You'll study how it has changed and why.

Inspect the photographs in figures 2-5 through 2-10, or bring in other pictures of old cars or gas stations. Perhaps you have a photograph of your mom's or dad's first car. Describe what you see. Compare and contrast the stations.

> In small study groups, select one photograph and research it at the library or on the Internet. Find out what major events were occurring at the time the photograph was taken. Who was president? Was America at war? What were the accomplishments of the era? What was life like for Americans?
>
> Write a newspaper article or stage a news broadcast as if it were happening then. Include indications of how the automobile influenced society at that time. You and your classmates will be the reporters, radio or TV anchors, and share what you find out.

In the century or so since its invention, the automobile has significantly influenced our way of life. In your small group, brainstorm several ways that gas stations and their architecture have changed and evolved over the years.

> List architectural structures other than gas stations that were created to meet the needs of the automobile culture. Share your list with the class. Select one structure and research it. Prepare a presentation with visual aids and a display that tells the story of your structure's beginning and ways it changed over time.
>
> Explain any connections your family had with any aspect of the automobile industry. Create a photograph essay on any example you find in your community.

CONSTRUCTION
MORE ARCHITECTURAL ADVENTURES

Architecture Everywhere, © 2000 Zephyr Press, Tucson, Arizona

DRIVE-INS— PAST, PRESENT, AND FUTURE

DESIGN

MAIN IDEAS IN THIS SECTION

- The automobile contributed to our mobile society.
- Drive-in architecture arose to cater to people on the move.
- Movement, speed, fun, cars, friends, food, good times are symbolized by logos, signs, colors, and shapes that appeal to the patrons in cars on the move.

MATERIALS

▶ figures 2-11 through 2-13 (see page 58 for enlarged photos)

FIGURE 2-11

FIGURE 2-12

FIGURE 2-13

OPTIONAL MATERIALS

▶ other photographs of drive-ins collected from older magazines (perhaps from used bookstores or library sales)

BLUEPRINTS
DRIVE-INS—PAST, PRESENT, AND FUTURE

Photocopy the following and pass it out to students, read it aloud to them, or use your own way of getting the concepts across to them:

Most of us think of McDonald's with its golden arches as the standard drive-in, fast-food restaurant. But it was in California in the 1930s that the drive-in form of architecture was invented. Included were restaurants, theaters, dry cleaners, supermarkets, banks, and film processing huts. Strip malls—stores built next to each other in a long, narrow strip— eventually came along, too.

Drive-ins and strip malls are built where traffic patterns intersect transportation routes. They reflect the needs of a mobile society.

But within the drive-in architectural style are many unique looks. The appearance of drive-ins reflects the fashions of the day and place. In the Southwest, the Pueblo style is popular. In the Southeast and California, the Spanish style—with arches and large, half-rounded windows—is favored. The colonial style is used in the East and Mid-Atlantic states. The Midwest is open to many styles—art deco, Tudor, and modern. But one thing all types have in common: Since the automobile travels rapidly, drive-ins and strip malls all require large electric signs that catch the attention of the driver or passengers.

Although you may not have your driver's license yet, you soon may be getting it. Look at the photographs in figures 2-11 through 2-13. Research drive-ins that were once in your community but are no longer. Find pictures of them in old newspapers or magazines, or from businesspeople. Compare them to the drive-ins you go to. Prepare a classroom exhibit that shows the evolution.

Think about how we use the automobile every day. Take an inventory of all the drive-in buildings or structures found in your community. Include not only fast-food restaurants but also banks, dry cleaners, post offices, supermarkets, and theaters. What do they look like and how are they built? What type of signage, lights, colors, and materials are used to appeal to people on the move?

> If you could design or redesign a drive-in building for the future, what would it be? What would it look like—what type of signage, colors, shapes, forms, and patterns would you use to attract the public? Using materials that might be available in the future or building materials that create a nostalgic reminder of the past, design a new chain of drive-ins that would be used by the people of the twenty-first century. Will you still be relying on the automobile, or some other means of transportation? Draw or write about your drive-in.

CONSTRUCTION

MORE ARCHITECTURAL ADVENTURES

CONSTRUCTION

MORE ARCHITECTURAL ADVENTURES

2-1: MAIN STREET, USA: YESTERDAY, TODAY, AND TOMORROW

Main streets have been the place of activity for the American city, town, or village. They have changed over the years. Does your town or city still have a busy main street that is the center of activity? Is it in good repair or in need of some attention?

Step 1. Find the area that you think was the original main street of your town.

Step 2. Use pencils, markers, or pens to draw what you see there now. Use your knowledge of one- and two-point perspective to capture the street from various angles and directions.

Step 3. Find at least three old photographs of the main street that represent three different times, if possible. Track the changes that have occurred.

Step 4. If you were an architect or designer, how would you change this main street to make it a current center of activity or to improve its appearance and usefulness to the community? Draw your ideal main street.

Your city library or government buildings are not only a source of information for the history of your area, but they might also be interested in displaying your designs.

2-2: CAPTURING ARCHITECTURAL DETAILS

Often the casual observer overlooks the small details of a building. However, these details reveal much. Select a building you find interesting. With your camera, take a shot of the entire structure, and then capture the details with a close-up lens if you have one. Arrange the photographs in a composition and glue them to foam board. On the back, print the name of the building, its age, style, and location. See if the class can locate the building and listen for their comments. You will probably hear such statements as "I've never seen that before."

2-3: JOBS MY ANCESTORS HAD AND WHAT A FINE PLACE OF EMPLOYMENT

Search your family tree or family fact sheet for the various occupations that your ancestors or immediate family members have had.

Step 1. Interview older relatives, friends, and neighbors about the kinds of jobs they have had and the places they did them. List these jobs from the present to as far back as you can trace them. Include buildings where they went to work. Were any of these jobs in your community?

Step 2. Based on what you know about current employment situations, speculate on what the following were like for your older relatives when they began working:

> *wages*
>
> *working conditions*
>
> *vacations*
>
> *hours per week on the job*
>
> *getting to and from work*
>
> *medical, dental, or other insurance*
>
> *annual bonus*
>
> *other company benefits*

Step 3. Ask the people you interviewed about the items on your list. How did their working conditions compare with those of today? Which answers confirmed your speculations? Which ones surprised you?

Step 4. Take or get photographs of the structures where your elders worked; factories, farms, office buildings, mines, banks, stores, mechanic shops are just a few examples you may find. If possible, locate tools of their trades, uniforms, or other artifacts from various eras of their employment.

Step 5. Prepare an illustrated written report. Present your information to the class.

2-4: THE HOMESTEAD: DID YOUR FAMILY HAVE ONE?

A homestead is the ancestral home or the place that was settled by the first of your ancestors to come to an area. Homesteads can be grand or very simple. Talk with your parents to find out where your family settled. Research and find photographs of your family's homestead. Write and present a report on your family's place to your class. Save the report, as it will be a treasure for you and your future family.

Architecture Everywhere, © 2000 Zephyr Press, Tucson, Arizona

2-5: HOW THE FARM HAS CHANGED: A DOCUMENTARY ON PROGRESS

Farms have a rich architectural history. The farmhouse, barns, machine sheds, chicken coops, pig pens, grain bins, and silos were at one time standard parts of farm architecture. Do you live on a farm? If you do, no doubt you have heard from your parents or relatives how the farm has changed. It is not a place where only intense manual labor takes place anymore, but one where computers and high technology play a large role. Document how your farm has changed. Your local Farm Bureau may be a source of information. Collect photographs and mount them in a scrapbook for your classmates to see. Keep the book for your descendants.

2-6: TRACKING IT DOWN: CHANGES IN TYPES OF ARCHITECTURE OVER TIME

Using your camera or camcorder, trace how a given type of architecture (church, hospital, school, movie theater, or some other type of building) in your community has changed over time. Often the buildings you have studied have records of various events that might help you understand the people who lived at different times. Investigate the feelings and thoughts of people as they relate to the buildings of various times. Some research sources are old diaries, letters, poems, centennial yearbooks, personal interviews, newspaper clippings, or microfiche of old newspapers. Prepare a presentation that illustrates and communicates what you have found out about the changes in both the buildings and the people.

2-7: IMAGE AND THE AUTOMOBILE AGE: A TIME LINE

Over the years, the automobile industry has provided us with some rich logos, images of speed, a type of class, expressions of form and function in various materials, and a variety of automobile colors that appeal to us. Collect old magazines that depict automobiles of all different types. Cover as wide a time span as possible. Cut out ads and pictures of a variety of cars, logos, accessories, and people who drive these cars. Now find pictures of various buildings that correspond to the eras of the cars. For example, a 1957 Chevy might be at a Big Boy drive-in restaurant, while a 1999 Ford Explorer might be parked next to a mountain cabin. Use the pictures to create an illustrated time line to show your findings.

2-8: GET YOUR KICKS ON ROUTE 66

America has many highways. Route 66, from Chicago to Los Angeles, was very popular in the 1950s and early 1960s, and is perhaps one of the most famous. There are many books about this highway. Get a map of the United States or individual maps from the states through which Route 66 travels. With a colored marker, outline the route of the highway.

Some examples of architecture that would be found along this or other highways would be gas stations, roadside restaurants or diners, rest stops, drive-ins, tourist cabins, motels, travel lodges, and roadside stands. To capture the time and unique architectural features of this mobile age, find magazine pictures or take color or black-and-white photographs of these types of structures. Attach your photographs along Route 66 on your highlighted map and display the map in your classroom.

2-9: AUTOMOBILES AND ARCHITECTURE OF THE FUTURE

Cars and trucks are essential for life today and most likely will be in the future as well. What will our need and love for the automobile create in the future? With your class, design a future community where the needs of the automobile will be integrated into the plan and architecture of the community by following these steps:

Step 1. Download from the Internet pictures of some cars that have competed in the annual Sunrayce. What is the source of power for these cars? Why is the race held during the month of June? What are other potential power sources for cars? If our future cars look similar to these, what changes would take place in the architecture of buildings designed to serve the needs of people in these cars?

Step 2. In small groups, select one type of building that currently caters to our mobile society (drive-through fast food, mall, gas station, car wash, drive-up bank ATMs). With your group, create a new design of that building with the car of the future in mind.

Step 3. Put your projects together into a class design of a new community that takes into account environmental impacts and that keeps the needs of the people in mind. Before you begin, agree on a scale (for example, 1 inch = 1 foot). Each group will construct its own new building, and the class will also create highways, parks, recreational areas—whatever you think will be needed in a community of the future that is dependent on the automobile for transportation. Use foam board, poster board, balsa wood, self-hardening clay, or other materials.

2-10: A Documentary on the Automobile Architecture in My City

The architecture of automobile dealerships is very interesting. Investigate various types of dealerships in your community. Originally cars for sale were placed in store-front windows. These stores and later dealerships were on the main streets of most American cities. Gradually the dealerships were placed on street corners next to new buildings where the dealers could place more cars for viewing. People built new dealerships that reflected the architectural styles popular at the time or reflected the image of the automobile itself. What old dealerships still remain in your city? Compare these to the new ones that require many acres near interstate highways or at the edges of town. How are the new dealerships built? Prepare a visual report with photographs or pictures from newspapers or magazines.

2-11: The 50s and the Drive-Ins

The 1950s were the decade of rock and roll, cars with fish tails, and girls who wore poodle skirts, bobby socks, and oxford shoes. It was also the time of the drive-ins. Interview people who were teenagers in the 1950s to find out about the drive-ins in their area and their experiences with them. Ask them why they think drive-ins were so popular. Read books, newspapers, or magazine articles from the decade to discover what the media had to say about drive-ins. Inventory various drive-ins that you have researched. Accompany this research with pictures or posters of the drive-ins.

2-12: A Photograph Essay of Our Town's Drive-Ins

After taking an inventory of all of the drive-ins in your community, select several that appeal to you. With a camera or camcorder, create a visual essay of these structures. Capture not only the building itself but also the details. Photograph or videotape these buildings when you have good light that provides contrast so you can highlight forms, textures, and surfaces of the buildings. Don't forget the signs. Organize your display in the hallway or classroom. Local public buildings such as the library or city hall also display students' work.

2-13: A Design for a Twenty-First Century Drive-in

I am your client. I want you, as my architect and designer, to create a new drive-in facility for my chain of fast-food restaurants. This chain of restaurants will be in outer space where we have several developing communities. You must provide the following:

a description of the type of restaurant you have created for me

a colored sketch of the outside and inside of the restaurant

a three-dimensional model

swatches of colors and fabrics you will use

a sketch of the logo

a menu

a sketch or completed uniform for the workers

I am open to any and all ideas as long as they are in good taste and affordable.

2-14: IMAGE AND THE AUTOMOBILE AGE

Image is associated with almost everything today. Some designers have created clothing that reflects a certain look and personality and they succeed in attracting certain personalities to their style. Designer clothing is often expensive and very popular.

Automobiles and their designs have similar personalities that attract certain buyers. If you remember, not too long ago, Saturn and Lexus as well as others targeted a specific segment of the population. Some of their considerations may have been the potential customer's budget, attitude, and interests (cost, safety, comfort, appearance, look, use). Your challenge is to create a new type of automobile that has been designed for the population you choose by following these steps:

Step 1. Decide whether to work alone or with a team.

Step 2. Choose your target customer (sex, age, economic status, interests).

Step 3. Sketch the new car or other vehicle.

Step 4. Use self-hardening clay to create a three-dimensional model of the car.

Step 5. Design a plan for the dealership, the building where your car will be sold. The logo, corporate colors, signage, and advertising slogan should reflect your new line of automobile.

Step 6. When your cars and dealerships are ready, bring them to the class auto exposition, where they will be displayed. As your classmates circulate through the exhibit, you will "pitch" your car as if they were the type of customer you had in mind when you began your project.

Unit 2
Photos

▲ FIGURE 2-1. WHEN DO YOU THINK THIS MAIN STREET WAS A BUSY
SHOPPING AREA? HOW DID YOU REACH THAT CONCLUSION?

▶ FIGURE 2-2. AFTER GENERAL STORES
WERE BUILT, SPECIALTY SHOPS APPEARED
ALONG MAIN STREETS IN THE 1920S.
THIS ONE IS IN CASCADE, IDAHO. (PHOTO
COURTESY OF THE RUSSELL LEE
COLLECTION, LIBRARY OF CONGRESS)

▲ FIGURE 2-3. BUILDINGS HAVE AN IMPORTANT AND LASTING IMPACT ON
HUMAN BEINGS. THIS DEPARTMENT STORE WAS DESIGNED BY ONE OF
AMERICA'S MOST FAMOUS ARCHITECTS. IT IS IN CHICAGO, ILLINOIS.
FIND OUT WHO DESIGNED IT.

▲ FIGURE 2-4. TODAY, MANY PEOPLE SHOP AT LOCAL DISCOUNT CENTERS AND MALLS.
LIST AT LEAST THREE REASONS THAT MALLS ARE SO POPULAR.

◀ *FIGURE 2-5. THIS FILLING
STATION WAS BUILT AROUND
1900. (PHOTO COURTESY OF
AMOCO OIL COMPANY)*

◀ *FIGURE 2-6. FIND THE ROYAL
CROWN ON TOP OF THE PUMP IN
THIS 1920S SPANISH-STYLE GAS
STATION. NOTICE THE CARS AND
THE CLOTHES THE PEOPLE ARE
WEARING. (PHOTO COURTESY OF
AMOCO OIL COMPANY)*

◀ *FIGURE 2-7. THIS TWO-BAY,
PORCELAIN-BOX STYLED GAS
STATION WAS TYPICAL OF THE
1950S AND 1960S. NOTICE
HOW THE PUMPS, AS WELL AS THE
STANDARD OIL SYMBOL, ARE
DIFFERENT FROM THOSE OF TODAY.
(PHOTO COURTESY OF AMOCO OIL
COMPANY)*

Architecture Everywhere, © 2000 Zephyr Press, Tucson, Arizona

FIGURE 2-8. IN WHAT YEAR WAS THIS FULL-SERVICE GAS STATION PHOTOGRAPHED? HOW CAN YOU TELL? (PHOTO COURTESY OF SHELL OIL COMPANY)

FIGURE 2-9. A TYPICAL 1990S SELF-SERVICE GAS STATION WITH A CONVENIENCE MART SIMILAR TO THE ONE THAT BEGAN TO APPEAR IN THE EARLY 1900S. (PHOTO COURTESY OF AMOCO OIL COMPANY)

FIGURE 2-10. HOW MANY TYPES OF STORES WOULD YOU FIND IN A CONTEMPORARY SHOPPING MALL THAT YOU WOULD NOT HAVE FOUND THIRTY YEARS AGO? WHAT MEANS DO MERCHANTS USE TO ATTRACT YOUR ATTENTION?

FIGURE 2-11. THIS TYPE OF DRIVE-IN FAST-FOOD RESTAURANT WAS INVENTED IN THE 1950S AND CONTINUES TO BE VERY POPULAR ALL ACROSS AMERICA AND THE WORLD.

FIGURE 2-12. THIS A&W RESTAURANT STILL HAS SERVERS WHO COME TO YOUR CAR AFTER YOU PLACE YOUR ORDER AT THE SPEAKER.

FIGURE 2-13. RETRO OR OLD-STYLE DRIVE-IN RESTAURANTS ARE VERY POPULAR TODAY. HERE IS A RECENT DRIVE-IN FROZEN CUSTARD STAND BUILT IN A 1950S STYLE. WHAT ELEMENTS MAKE UP THAT LOOK?

Architecture Everywhere, © 2000 Zephyr Press, Tucson, Arizona

Unit 3
What Our Ancestors Left Us
Cultural Groups and Their Building Traditions

When a style is found to be original and vital it is a certainty that it has sprung from the needs of the plain people and that it is based upon the simplest and most direct principles of construction.

—Gustav Stickley

FOUNDATION

IN THIS UNIT, STUDENTS

- ■ IDENTIFY THEIR OWN AND CLASSMATES' BACKGROUNDS AND FAMILIES' COUNTRIES OF ORIGIN.

- ■ RESEARCH NATIVE AMERICAN ARCHITECTURE AND EVALUATE THE TYPE, PURPOSE, AND CHARACTERISTICS OF EACH REGION'S BUILDINGS.

- ■ DEFINE AND RECOGNIZE CULTURAL AND VERNACULAR ARCHITECTURAL DESIGNS CREATED BY CERTAIN GROUPS.

Photocopy the following and pass it out to students, read it aloud to them, or use your own way of getting the concepts across to them:

You have learned about family ties. Unless you are a Native American, you have roots in other countries. For example, you might have an Italian great-grandfather who came to America and brought his Italian heritage and customs with him: his use of the Italian language, his religious beliefs and practices, his tastes for Italian food and drink, and his skills or crafts to make a living. The home he built and the materials he used to construct it may have been expressions of American ideas and Italian aesthetic preferences, technology, and craftsmanship.

American buildings, like other parts of our culture, are a combination of ideas that reflect cultural diversity. This diversity is played out in the crafts, workmanship, technical knowledge, and aesthetics of each group that settled in the United States. For example, the Spanish brought their use of stucco and tile, and the *loggia,* or covered porch. Each group used its buildings not only as shelter and a place to work, but also as an expression of their cultural heritage. The religious, social, or political ideas of these people were addressed imaginatively and aesthetically through a variety of building types. As a result, we can study people and learn more about their cultural traditions through the buildings found in each geographical region of the United States.

EXPLORING CULTURE

DESIGN

MAIN IDEAS IN THIS SECTION

- Native Americans were the first residents of our land. Everyone else has origins in other countries.
- Like the United States in general, a classroom is a composite of people who contribute in interesting ways to make America diverse and rich.
- People can research their roots by using primary sources (diaries, letters, journals, family histories, interviews with older family members, records).
- The classroom is a place for displaying projects and productions that contribute to our understanding of one another's origins and backgrounds.

MATERIALS

- ▶ a large map of the world to post on a bulletin board
- ▶ a large map of the United States to post
- ▶ push-pins with colored heads
- ▶ narrow colored ribbon

GUIDELINES FOR INSTRUCTION

If your classroom is ethnically and culturally mixed, use the passage in the blueprints section to guide students to identify the ethnic roots of various surnames. If your class is homogeneous, provide ethnically diverse names of authors, sports figures, pop singers, celebrities, or others. Ask the class to determine why you brought in these names. Guide the discussion in a way that values and appreciates the diversity in the class and in our country.

BLUEPRINTS
EXPLORING CULTURE

Photocopy the following section for students to read or read it aloud to them.

Think about the last names of your classmates. What do the names reveal about their ethnic origin? Unless you are a Native American, you have roots in parts of the world other than the United States. Before you explore the building traditions of your ancestors, find out more about you and your classmates' cultural connections. When we know something about the customs and traditions of people, we understand what they find beautiful and how their opinions influence American culture, particularly architecture.

Talk to your parents, grandparents, and other older relatives and get all the information you can about your family's country of origin and places of migration. You may have to go back many generations, or just a few, depending on when they came to the United States. Ask them about the following:

the origin of your family name and any changes it has undergone

the reasons your ancestors came to the United States

the place they first arrived

the places they went after wars

property they owned

their occupations

If you are Native American, you might find more information in tribal records.

Bring the information you find out to class. If you are not Native American, on a large class map of the world, mark your ancestors' countries of origin with small map pins. Mark the places where they entered the United States with other pins. If you are Native American, you'll mark an area of the United States, and mark areas where your ancestors traveled to end up where you are now. Connect the pins with pieces of colored ribbon. When all the journeys have been mapped, stand back and admire the gift that makes our country so interesting and diverse.

RESOURCE SHELF

▶ relatives

▶ genealogy groups

▶ cultural history museums, groups, or societies

▶ federal Bureau of Indian Affairs

▶ Internet

CONSTRUCTION
MORE ARCHITECTURAL ADVENTURES

Architecture Everywhere, © 2000 Zephyr Press, Tucson, Arizona

THE FIRST AMERICAN ARCHITECTS AND BUILDERS

DESIGN

MAIN IDEAS IN THIS SECTION

- Native Americans have a long, rich history and tradition of architecture.
- Various regions of the country were and are home to various tribes. Available materials and climate shape building construction.
- Each group represented its beliefs symbolically, incorporating symbolic images in their buildings.

MATERIALS

▶ figures 3-1 through 3-5 (see pages 74–75 for enlarged photos)

FIGURE 3-1

FIGURE 3-2

FIGURE 3-3

FIGURE 3-4

FIGURE 3-5

BLUEPRINTS
THE FIRST AMERICAN ARCHITECTS AND BUILDERS

Photocopy the following and pass it out to students, read it aloud to them, or use your own way of getting the concepts across to them:

Native American architecture was in place years before the arrival of Christopher Columbus. Native American people handed down their building traditions for centuries. Approximately three hundred Native American groups created and continue to create a variety of structures all over North America. Each has specific design and construction techniques depending on the purpose and function of the buildings, and on the materials available.

Many Native American groups have buildings for a variety of seasonal uses: storage and work, religious and council functions, and sleeping and raising families. These structures are built and arranged in consistent patterns that reflect the social functions of the group. One such example is the pueblo (see figure 3-1), built in the Southwest.

Just as elsewhere, the design and appearance of individual buildings are shaped by a combination of factors. What effects do you think weather and climate, available materials, and the social functions and lifestyles of the group have on the design of each building?

There are as many different styles of original American architecture as there are Native American groups. Some architectural types are hundreds of years old, while others are as recent as the nineteenth century. Each region of the United States, including the Hawaiian Islands and Alaska, has structures built by the people who originally lived there. Look at figures 3-2 through 3-5. These drawings and the photograph depict types of Native American architecture. Each is found in a different region of the United States, and each was designed by the nation, tribe, or group who lived there. Find out which building was built by which group. Of the four drawings, which example is the oldest? When was it constructed? Where in the United States would you find it? Following are some clues to help you identify the buildings:

- Think of weather as a factor that affected the design and function of each.
- Determine the material used for the structures.
- Note that the oldest one still exists, and you can visit it.

Each tribe has unique building traditions. Select a region and study the peoples who lived or live there. Investigate customs, beliefs, celebrations, and lifestyles. Analyze how the architecture reflected or reflects an important part of their lifestyle and community. Keep in mind that, after the Europeans arrived, groups were often forced to move to land or reservations in regions other than those in which they originally lived. You may need to trace such movements. Locate reproductions of drawings, paintings, or photographs of important people in the group's history. Create a display, model community, drawings, essay, or other means of presenting your findings to your class.

Architecture Everywhere, © 2000 Zephyr Press, Tucson, Arizona

Resource Shelf

▶ library
▶ Internet
▶ historical societies
▶ state historical archives
▶ tribal publications, tapes, and videos
▶ the work of American artists such as George Catlin

CONSTRUCTION
More Architectural Adventures

See next section, page 69.

IDEAS FROM AFRICA, CHINA, AND EUROPE ADD TO AMERICAN ARCHITECTURE

DESIGN

MAIN IDEAS IN THIS SECTION

- All people who came to live in America brought an approach to building that incorporated elements and traditions from their homeland.
- Vernacular architecture is a combination of traditional elements coupled with materials available and other styles found in the new land.
- Certain crafts with specific materials are associated with specific groups.

MATERIALS

▶ figures 3-6 through 3-11 (see pages 76–77 for enlarged photos)

FIGURE 3-6

FIGURE 3-7

FIGURE 3-8

FIGURE 3-9

FIGURE 3-10

FIGURE 3-11

MATERIALS

► figures 3-12 through 3-15A (see pages 78–80 for enlarged photos)

FIGURE 3-12

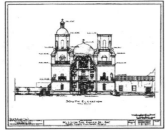
FIGURE 3-13

FIGURE 3-14

FIGURE 3-15

FIGURE 3-15A

GUIDELINES FOR INSTRUCTION

If possible, locate styles of buildings that reflect students' ancestral traditions. Perhaps there are examples in your community.

BLUEPRINTS
IDEAS FROM AFRICA, CHINA, AND EUROPE ADD TO AMERICAN ARCHITECTURE

Photocopy the following section for students to read or read it aloud to them.

Every immigrant group that settled in America brought with it many cultural values from its native country. As we have discovered, approaches to building or architectural design were among these elements. Therefore, across America we can find lasting, visual reminders of our immigrant ancestors in buildings. Homes, churches, meeting houses, or civic buildings are just a few examples. You are going to study some of the special buildings, designs, and craftsmanship in which your ancestors excelled. There may be local examples of these buildings still standing. You know the place in the United States where your family first arrived, and you know something about your city and the people who settled it. Your next adventure is to find out what special designs or construction materials these people used.

When immigrants built a building or hired an architect to design a building using plans found in pattern books or based on the designs of a known architect, we call the resulting style *pure style*. (We will study styles in unit 4.) When immigrant groups used design elements from their homeland and materials at hand, the result was called *vernacular architecture*. The term *vernacular* suggests a combination of ingenuity, special traditional cultural designs, and skill in construction. Figure 3-6 is an example of vernacular architecture. In the United States, many examples of vernacular buildings still exist. Perhaps you have some in your community. You are going to learn about them, their themes, and the people who built them.

RESOURCE SHELF

▶ local historical societies

▶ state and local historical preservation commissions

▶ county courthouse for information about the sale of land and property, dates, and improvements made to buildings

Photocopy the following section for students to read or read it aloud to them.

There are many immigrant groups in the United States—German, Irish, Italian, Swedish, Japanese, French, Russian, Danish, Ukraine, Finnish, Belgian, Dutch, Swiss, Mexican, Caribbean, Czech, Portuguese, to name only a few. Each group brought something unique to American architecture. Some characteristics that reflect the culture are found in their homes, barns, churches, and other buildings. Some specialize in using wood; others, stone, stucco, or brick. Some excel in their use of metal and forging; others in using plaster and moldings. Some groups were known for their wood carving; others, for their fresco painting. Some were skilled in their ability to create fabulous carved plaster ceilings; others cut stone and carved figures into stone. Your research will reveal much about various people and what they built. For example, if you have ever been to Williamsburg, Virginia, you know that English builders used their traditional crafts to build the entire town.

Look at figures 3-7 through 3-15A, which are examples of buildings constructed by African, English, Spanish, and Chinese builders who came to the United States. Compare and contrast the location, shape, material, size, roof, doors, and windows of the buildings. What visual clues help you determine which group constructed which buildings?

Where are there examples of these types of architecture in your community? Study them to determine the age of the buildings.

RESOURCE SHELF

- ▶ builders
- ▶ factory owners
- ▶ union representatives
- ▶ organizations that specialize in information on the work of immigrant groups
- ▶ curators of museums
- ▶ archivists in state or local historical museums

CONSTRUCTION
MORE ARCHITECTURAL ADVENTURES

CONSTRUCTION

MORE ARCHITECTURAL ADVENTURES

3-1: MAPPING IMMIGRANT PATHS

Look at the map of you and your classmates' ancestors' journey to the United States. Whose ancestors traveled the greatest distance? The shortest?

3-2: A SPECIAL IMMIGRANT FAMILY

Many of our ancestors suffered great hardship to come to the United States, while others had an easier journey. Research an ancestor who came here from another country. If you cannot locate a family member, use one from a friend's or neighbor's family for the purpose of this research. Through oral history, diaries, letters, and photographs, gather information about the person:

- When and why did the person come to the United States? How did he or she travel here?
- Did any unusual events or difficult situations occur on the journey?
- What did the person do to earn a living when he or she first arrived?
- In what areas and in what types of buildings did the person live?
- To what religious group or ethnic organization did the person belong?

If you are African American or Native American, or if your ancestor came from a country that did not keep records or that had its records destroyed, you may have to rely on oral history for your research. Find out as much as you can by talking with your relatives. Prepare a report and illustrate it with drawings or photographs that depict various times, and present it to the class along with any artifacts or other personal items you find in your research.

3-3: CREATING A TIME LINE OF OUR IMMIGRANT FAMILIES

In unit 1, you used a clothesline and colored index cards or colored ink to show our city's history. Now you will add to that time line beginning with the people who settled the region in which you live. Research to prepare a list of the groups who immigrated to your community. Use different colored index cards or inks from those already on the time line, and add the new cards in their proper sequence.

3-4: CREATING AN EXHIBIT OF CULTURAL ARTIFACTS

In a small team, research specific groups that settled in your area. Each team should choose a different group. Ask community members or organizations if you may borrow artifacts and objects—tools, clothing, printed materials in the native language, photographs, personal objects, toys—associated with that group. Use the objects to create an exhibit. Arrange them in chronological order. Make a descriptive label for each item to identify its age, source, and purpose or other information. Many of these items are no doubt priceless or have great sentimental value. Be sure to put them on display in a secure place and return them after the exhibit.

3-5: NOT ALL WORK AND NO PLAY: WHAT NATIVE AMERICANS AND IMMIGRANTS DID FOR FUN

Sports and games are interesting to research because they show us how people relaxed or had fun when the work was done. Select one immigrant or Native American group and find out about their favorite pastimes. What outdoor games or sports did they play? What indoor games did they play? What else did they do to relax? In what structures did each of these activities take place? Teach your classmates how to play some of the games or activities.

3-7: THE MUSIC AND DANCE OF OUR ANCESTORS

Music, dance, poetry, and literature express the ideas a particular people have about life. Select a group that reflects your family's culture. Then select one or two art forms and research how they reflect what is unique about your culture. Share your research with the class by playing the music, performing the dance, reading the poetry, or displaying the artwork.

3-8: SET THE STAGE: A PLAY ABOUT OUR COMMUNITY AND ITS TRADITIONS

After you have sufficient information on the life and traditions of several groups, divide into small performance troupes in your class. Each troupe will choose a different group. Use stories from diaries, biographies, legends, and songs to create a play about these people and the place they came from. You might include folk dances or stories that reflect the time, mood, and people. Use your own imagination. Write a script or improvise using the information you gather. A narrator can read it or you can pantomime. Record your production on videotape, if possible, as you present it to the class or to the school.

3-9: THE BUILDING TRADITIONS OF AMERICANS

This unit has introduced you to many different groups who live in the United States. You've learned about the group's unique approach to designing buildings. Select one group that you are particularly interested in, either because you are part of that group in some way or for another reason. Research the group's architectural styles, construction techniques, and aesthetic elements. Analyze the construction innovations the group brought to or created in the United States. How and why did the features travel to various areas in the United States? For example, African Americans incorporated the full front porch. Prepare charts, drawings, and posters that depict what you find in your research.

3-10: CAPTURING AND RECORDING ORAL HISTORIES ABOUT BUILDING TRADITIONS

With a camcorder or camera, prepare a visual record of examples of architecture found in your community. Others may have already done this research, and there may even be photographs, but using your own will be more exciting. Ask senior citizens in your community what they remember about these structures, and tape record their answers. Present your pictures and tapes to the class.

3-11: COMPARING AND CONTRASTING THE MOTHERLAND AND THE NEW LAND

To appreciate the contribution our ancestors made to architecture in the United States, study the types of architectural styles found in their countries of origin. You can find this information in a resource book on world architecture or on the Internet. In some countries, architectural design has been developing and changing for centuries. Identify the major styles and materials for which they are most famous. Compare and contrast these examples to those in the United States that were built by the corresponding group. Present this information in an oral report with visual aids.

3-12: CREATING A MODEL OF A SETTLEMENT

Working with a team, select any ethnic group you want. Use the information you gathered in this unit to create a realistic three-dimensional model of an imaginary or actual settlement. Select the year, place, and types of buildings you will incorporate. Build the model to scale to achieve a sense of realism. Use objects you find, natural materials, and toys or materials from hobby stores such as those used in model railroads. Display the finished settlements in the media center or classroom.

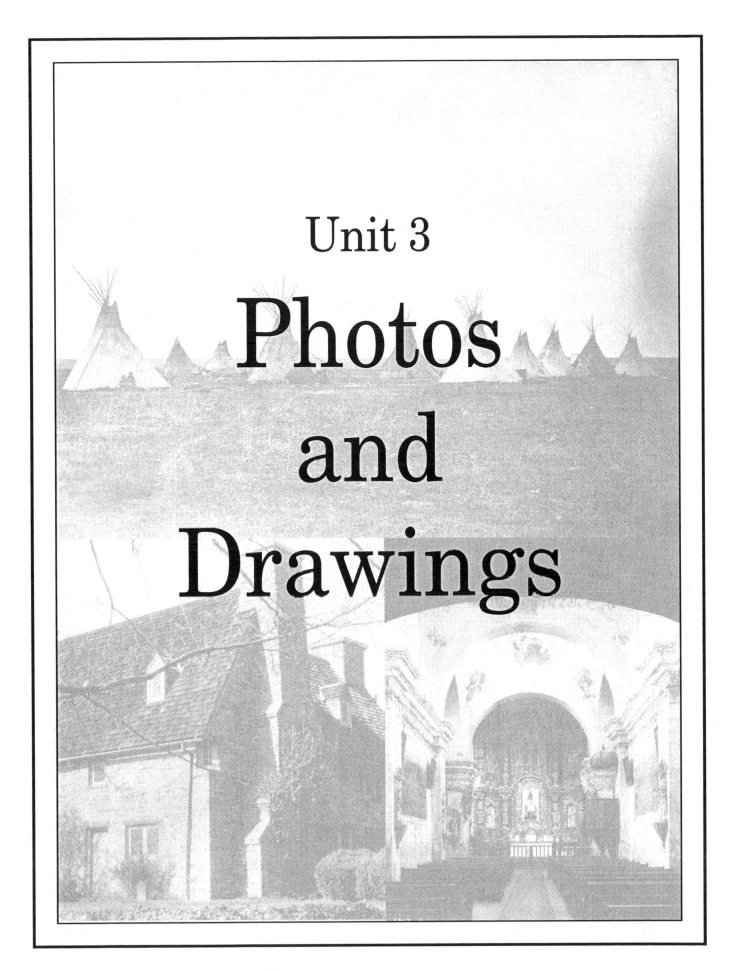

Unit 3

Photos
and
Drawings

FIGURE 3-1. TAOS PUEBLO IS AN EXAMPLE OF A COMMUNAL DWELLING FIRST BUILT IN 1540 AND REBUILT IN 1700. THIS PUEBLO CAN BE FOUND IN TAOS, NEW MEXICO. WHAT ARE THE ROUND OBJECTS NEAR THIS PUEBLO? (PHOTO BY E. KIDDER SMITH)

FIGURE 3-2. THIS COMMUNITY WAS SETTLED CIRCA 900. WHAT WAS THE PURPOSE OF BUILDING ON A MOUND? IN 1259, THIS COMMUNITY OF MOUND BUILDERS NUMBERED AROUND 30,000 INHABITANTS. IN 1400, THE POPULATION BEGAN TO DECLINE. WHY? (DRAWING BY JOHN ADKINS RICHARDSON, © 1992, ARRESSICO)

FIGURE 3-3. A LARGE HOME SUCH AS THIS ONE COULD HOUSE FIVE OR SIX FAMILIES. WHERE DID THIS TRIBE LIVE? WHAT IS THE NAME GIVEN TO THIS TYPE OF BUILDING?

▲ FIGURE 3-4. THIS IS AN EXAMPLE OF A CHIEF'S HOUSE. WHERE WOULD YOU FIND THIS TYPE OF BUILDING? WHAT DO THE DESIGNS PAINTED ON THE HOUSE REPRESENT? WHAT IS THE SIGNIFICANCE OF THE POLE IN FRONT?

▲ FIGURE 3-5. IN WHAT PART OF THE UNITED STATES WOULD YOU FIND THESE MOVABLE HOUSES? WHAT ARE THEY CALLED? WHERE DO YOU SEE CHILDREN IN THE PHOTOGRAPH? (PHOTO COURTESY OF THE SMITHSONIAN INSTITUTION, WASHINGTON, D.C.)

FIGURE 3-6. THE FRENCH BUILT HOUSES AND CHURCHES SUCH AS THESE IN THE EIGHTEENTH CENTURY ALONG THE MISSISSIPPI VALLEY. THIS STRUCTURE WAS FIRST BUILT IN 1737 AS A HOUSE AND LATER SERVED AS A COURTHOUSE IN CAHOKIA, ILLINOIS. THE BUILDERS USED A TECHNIQUE CALLED PORTEAU EN TERRE, OR "POST SET VERTICALLY IN THE EARTH." THE PAVILION ROOFS FORM A GALLERY OR PORCH AROUND THE HOUSE.

FIGURE 3-7. THIS BUILDING IS STANDING IN AMERICA'S OLDEST CITY. WHERE IS IT? IT WAS BUILT BY THE SPANISH AND HAS A LOGGIA. WHAT IS A LOGGIA? WHAT IS STUCCO? (PHOTO COURTESY OF HABS)

FIGURE 3-8. THE HENRY WHITFIELD HOUSE WAS BUILT IN GUILDFORD, CONNECTICUT, IN 1639. WHAT IMMIGRANT GROUP BUILT IT? WHAT SPECIAL SKILLS IN BUILDING DID THEY HAVE?

► *FIGURE 3-9. WHAT GROUP BROUGHT THIS TYPE OF LONG AND NARROW CONSTRUCTION TO AMERICA? WHEN? WHAT SPECIAL ARCHITECTURAL FEATURES DID THIS GROUP CONTRIBUTE TO AMERICAN ARCHITECTURE? WHY IS THIS HOUSE CALLED A SHOTGUN HOUSE?*

► *FIGURE 3-10. HERE IS A FLOOR PLAN OF THE SHOTGUN HOUSE. WHY IS IT SO LONG AND NARROW?*

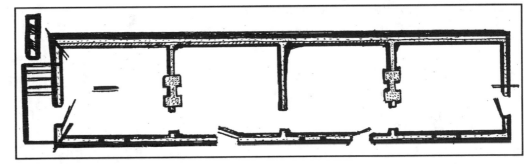

► *FIGURE 3-11. THIS IS CALLED THE YUNG SEE SAN FONG HOUSE. IT WAS ORIGINALLY BUILT IN 1916 OR 1917 IN LOS GATOS, CALIFORNIA. WHY IS IT SO BIG? WHAT ARCHITECTURAL FEATURES ARE REMINISCENT OF THE GROUP THAT BUILT IT? (PHOTO COURTESY OF HABS)*

FIGURE 3-12. ROW HOUSES WERE BUILT IN MANY MAJOR INDUSTRIAL CITIES IN AMERICA AND BECAME HOME TO MANY IRISH FAMILIES. WHAT DISTINGUISHES A ROW HOUSE FROM OTHER STYLES? WHAT MATERIALS WERE USED IN ITS CONSTRUCTION?

FIGURE 3-13. THIS IS AN EXAMPLE OF FACHWERK IN WHICH BRICKS WERE LAID BETWEEN SUPPORTING TIMBERS. NOTICE THE PATTERN OF THE BRICKS ON THE WALL AND THE GROUND. FROM WHAT COUNTRY DID THIS STYLE ORIGINATE? (PHOTO COURTESY OF E. KIDDER SMITH)

FIGURE 3-14. THIS IS AN EXAMPLE OF THE GERMAN HOUSE-BARN COMBINATION. WHAT BENEFITS AND DRAWBACKS WOULD THIS DESIGN CREATE FOR ITS INHABITANTS?

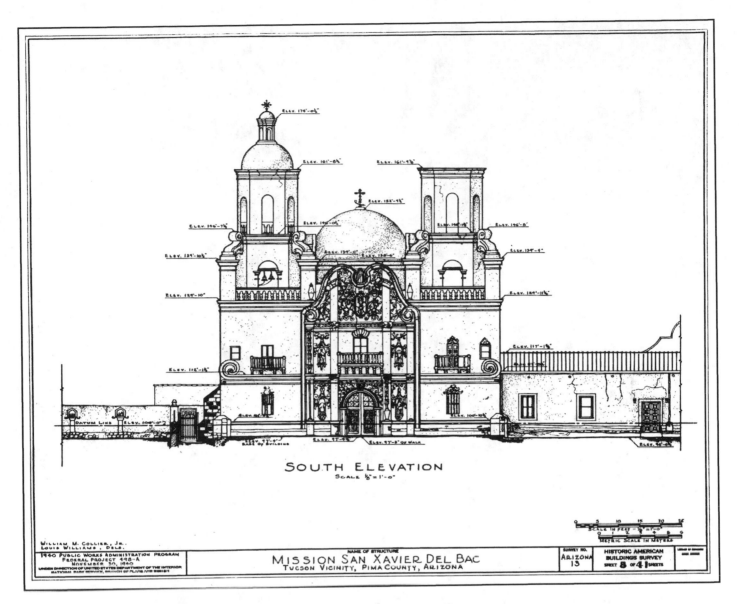

SOUTH ELEVATION
Scale ⅛" = 1'-0"

MISSION SAN XAVIER DEL BAC
Tucson Vicinity, Pima County, Arizona

▲ FIGURE 3-15. MISSION SAN XAVIER DEL BAC, NEAR TUCSON, ARIZONA, WITH ITS DOUBLE TOWERS AND
DOME, IS AN EXCELLENT EXAMPLE OF A LATE-EIGHTEENTH-CENTURY COLONIAL MEXICAN MISSION. THE
ENTRANCE FACADE IS RICHLY DECORATED. WHAT PURPOSE DID THE TOWERS SERVE? WHY WAS THE FACADE
SO ORNATE? (PHOTO COURTESY OF HABS)

▲ FIGURE 3-15A. THE INTERIOR OF MISSION SAN XAVIER DEL BAC IS PAINTED AND
CONTAINS CARVED SCREENS AND STATUES. WHAT EFFECT DOES THE HIGH CEILING
HAVE ON THE ACOUSTICS? (PHOTO COURTESY OF HABS)

Unit 4
Steps in Style

Now the progress which a people makes in any of the fine arts, must depend on public sensibility and the public taste. Sensibility to beauty must exist, and there must be some means afforded of developing and cultivating taste; for, however instinctive and natural a gift the former may be, a correct taste is only the result of education.

—A. J. Downing

FOUNDATION

IN THIS UNIT, STUDENTS

■ EXPLORE THE WAYS STYLES OF CONSTRUCTION HAVE CHANGED OVER TIME.

■ IDENTIFY THE CHARACTERISTICS OF VARIOUS STYLES IN AMERICAN ARCHITECTURE.

■ DISCOVER HOW TO DETERMINE THE AGE OF A BUILDING BY ITS CHARACTERISTICS.

■ STUDY AND COMPARE THE STYLES OF SEVERAL FAMOUS AMERICAN ARCHITECTS.

Photocopy the following and pass it out to students, read it aloud to them, or use your own way of getting the concepts across to them:

In unit 3, you learned that vernacular architecture was a combination of traditional approaches to building. In this unit you identify and research pure styles of architecture. These major groups are presented by style in sequence from the sixteenth century to the present. Pure styles are based primarily on architects' or designers' plans found in books. These plans incorporate certain principles, features, or aesthetic characteristics found in a given era, such as Greek revival. By studying the various pure styles and understanding the elements and characteristics of each, you can detect the period in which the building was constructed. You will also be able to identify buildings that are a combination of several styles and locate them easily in your community. In a sense you can become an architectural detective.

DEFINING STYLE

DESIGN

MAIN IDEAS IN THIS SECTION

- An architectural style is an overall plan with visual characteristics based on ideas or fashions popular during given periods.
- Styles change with new technologies, historical events, the economy, and the tastes of people, especially leaders.

MATERIALS

▶ figures 4-1 through 4-4 (see pages 112–113 for enlarged photos)

FIGURE 4-1

FIGURE 4-2

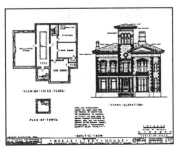

FIGURE 4-3

FIGURE 4-4

BLUEPRINTS
DEFINING STYLE

Photocopy the following section for students to read or read it aloud to them.

What is a style? A style is the way something is expressed or designed using specific elements, materials, and plans. In architecture, style refers to an overall plan that embodies certain visual characteristics found in buildings. These visual characteristics are based on ideas or fashions that were popular during certain historical eras. Various American architects and designers over the years have interpreted elements such as color, shape, pattern, balance, texture, mass, and form.

As with most fashions or styles, architectural designs change with time. These changes reflect new technologies, events in history, the economy, and the tasks of the people, especially in government. Designers, architects, or master craftspeople create such styles and then print them in books and magazines for the public. For example, architect Andrea Palladio (1508–1580) and designer and master craftsman Samuel McIntire are known for their contributions to American architecture. Thomas Jefferson also influenced American architecture. He favored the classical style that you see represented in many government buildings and used in the design of his own home Monticello. William Thornton used the classical style in his 1793 plan for the Capitol Building in Washington, D.C. (figure 4-1).

Italianate is another American architectural style, popular between 1840 and 1885. Used mainly in homes but found also in public buildings, it was influenced by Italian villas. These villas were usually asymmetrical, with a large tower on one end. The buildings constructed in this popular, romantic style were two or more stories surrounded by land or close to the sea. Pairs of windows were often long and arched at the top. The roofs were hipped and pitched low. The exterior building materials were wood, stone, and brick. Figure 4-2 is a good example of this style.

The Victorians loved decorative, massive, detailed structures. American architects and designers adapted this style for use in American houses and buildings. Figure 4-3 is an example of American Victorian architecture. It is of the front view of a house as well as a floor plan of the third floor.

American architecture has a wide range of styles within its boundaries. Some communities are much older than others and therefore have many more architectural styles. Each style reflects a given time. For example, the Italianate style used in the Henry Shaw house (figure 4-4) in St. Louis, Missouri, built in 1849, was also used in the Morris-Libby house (figure 4-2), in Portland, Maine, built in 1859.

> Look at figure 4-1, a photograph of the U.S. Capitol Building. Find a picture of the capitol building in your state and compare and contrast it to the one in the photograph. Are there any other buildings in your community that have a similar style? If so, what purposes do they serve?

Examine figure 4-3. Based on what you see in the plan for the third floor, what do you think was on the second and first floors? What use did the house's tower serve?

Why are the houses in figures 4-2 and 4-4 known by their names?

CONSTRUCTION

MORE ARCHITECTURAL ADVENTURES

4-1: Carving a Style in Time (page 100)

Architecture Everywhere, © 2000 Zephyr Press, Tucson, Arizona

Learning to Be an Architectural Detective

Design

Main Ideas in This Section

- Architects and designers follow specific principles to create certain functional yet beautiful styles of architecture that become popular and come to reflect given eras.
- With study and investigation, you can identify characteristics associated with these styles and locate examples in your community.
- Because it is an art, architecture is affected by various political, historical, and social issues and events.
- Architecture styles constantly change to reflect the times, fashions, and needs of the people it serves.

Materials

▶ figures 4-5 through 4-21 (see pages 114–122 for enlarged photos)

Optional Materials

▶ examples of American architecture

▶ calendars, posters, magazine pictures, videos, slides, and books

▶ definitions of terms from the glossary (page 206) that explain the characteristics of various styles

Guidelines for Instruction

This section is organized by time periods. With one exception, each era has at least one photograph that represents an architectural style of the era. All the photographs have some background information and characteristic features described. The questions that follow require thought, analysis, and in some cases, research. Allow time for students to explore these questions so they understand each style in depth. The remaining architectural adventures are at the end of the unit.

BLUEPRINTS
Learning to Be an Architectural Detective

Photocopy the following section for students to read or read it aloud to them.

Learning to read a piece of architecture is like learning to understand a work of art. Each has a history and is created at a certain time. Sometimes an architect, such as Frank Lloyd Wright, becomes famous for a particular style, use of material, or look. Architecture is a functional art form intended to serve the needs of the client. New technologies, materials, and construction techniques affect the ways an architect can design a building. People and events in local and world history affect our human-made environment as architects respond to these events. When you research American architectural styles, you plot America's aesthetic standards along a visual time line and come to understand what was popular at the time. This architectural heritage, like art, reflects who we are as a nation.

You have explored the architecture of Native Americans, the first builders in America, who created distinctive types of regional architecture. In this unit, you will examine the stages and kinds of architecture that developed in the United States from the earliest days until the present. You will discover that specific characteristics are reflected in certain architectural designs. Architects create these designs that leave a distinctive mark on the humanmade environment. These plans and designs become styles; that is, others duplicate them so they are repeated in many buildings in that era. Once you know the specific elements of the style, you can recognize them in buildings of that era. You can also determine the age of a given building by determining its style.

RESOURCE SHELF

▶ many buildings
▶ school and public libraries
▶ historical libraries
▶ organizations such as the American Institute of Architects
▶ Internet
▶ local preservation commissions or landmark associations
▶ National Trust for Historic Preservation

Photocopy the following section for students to read or read it aloud to them.

You are going to look at American architectural styles by era. This overview outlines the steps that styles of American architecture took to get where it is today. You will notice that some eras overlap, meaning they were still being used while newer styles were emerging. As a class, we will discuss some general characteristics of each group, and then you will find more specific information on your own. You will select styles to investigate that are found in your community or region. Look at the photographs in the figures and study the characteristics of each building. Think about and identify the specific elements in each example. In your research you will look for buildings in your community that exhibit those same elements or characteristics.

Architecture Everywhere, © 2000 Zephyr Press, Tucson, Arizona

THE EARLY YEARS

The earliest European settlers of the United States came with very few possessions. They often had only the clothes they were wearing and a few personal belongings. They brought their pets and working animals with them, too. If they had a trade in their country of origin, such as stone mason, joiner, or blacksmith, they brought the tools of that trade. Once they arrived, they built shelters for their animals and themselves. They had to build these shelters with materials available here, but they built these buildings in the style, shape, or appearance of those in the country they had left to remind them of their country of origin and to create a comfortable feeling of familiarity.

POST-MEDIEVAL ENGLISH, CIRCA 1600–1700 (FIGURE 4-5)

Found in New England, mid-atlantic, or southern coastal states, this style of building has two stories in northern states and one in southern states. It is marked by steeply pitched roofs and large chimneys in its center, and small casement windows with multiple panes. It is usually built of stone, wood siding, or brick. It is typically one room deep. Decorative, carved tops were often placed on top.

Speculate about why this type of architecture is found in these areas. Why is the roof steeply pitched? Where is the decorative top? What additional features can you identify? What purposes do you think these features served?

DUTCH COLONIAL, CIRCA 1625–1840 (FIGURES 4-6 AND 4-7)

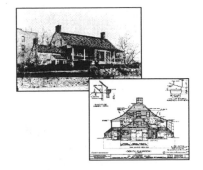
Found mainly in New York State, this style building has a gambreled roof (having several pitches on the front and back sides). It is marked by a Dutch front door with windows placed symmetrically on either side. It also usually had a separate bake house. It is usually built of stone, wood, or brick.

Speculate as to why this type of architecture is found in New York. What is a Dutch door? What purpose does it serve? Why is there a separate bake house? What additional features can you identify? What purposes do you think these features served?

GEORGIAN, CIRCA *1700–1780* (FIGURE *4-8*)

Based on designs by famous English architects such as Inigo Jones, Christopher Wren, and James Gibbs, settlers in Boston, Philadelphia, Annapolis, and Williamsburg brought this architectural style to the colonies. The style emphasizes classical details that grew out of the Italian Renaissance. It is found in homes, churches, and public meeting places. The plans were published in books, and variations of the Georgian look were adapted and constructed throughout the area.

What English kings inspired this style? What was the significance of the pineapple shape often added to this style of house? Have you seen it elsewhere? What are some other classical Renaissance features? What purposes do they serve?

FEDERAL, CIRCA *1780–1820* (FIGURE *4-9*)

Influenced by the *Federalists Papers,* this style was used in federal government buildings in Washington, D.C. Notice the fan and side-light windows in the front of the house. The style reflects Greek and Roman architecture. It was made popular by Thomas Jefferson.

What views expressed in the *Federalist Papers* are reflected in this building? What are keystones and where were they placed in buildings? What similarities do you see between the Georgian and federal styles? For what other reasons is Thomas Jefferson known? What other features do you notice? What purposes do they serve?

GREEK REVIVAL, CIRCA *1825–1860* (FIGURE *4-10*)

Used in a variety of buildings as a symbol of America's independence from other countries, this style has a very classic, grand, formal look. It borrows motifs from Greek architecture. It has a heavier feel than the federal style. It uses a temple form with pillars across the front, triangular pediments above the columns, and an entablature that creates a visual band or line to separate the columns from the pediment. It is white.

Architecture Everywhere, © 2000 Zephyr Press, Tucson, Arizona

What does "heavier feel" mean? What is an entablature? What three elements characterize it? Locate the plans of Asher Benjamin and Minard Lafever, two architects and designers who published their Greek revival plans for others to use. Evaluate the plans. Note how many of the elements in the plans were used in the building in the photograph. What purposes did these elements serve?

THE ROMANTIC AND VICTORIAN PERIODS

During this period, Americans discovered their own identity as a people and as a nation. They were interested in people and places that were far away, known through stories, newspaper articles, illustrations, and travelers' tales. The American West, Native Americans, nature, and adventure in exotic lands occupied their curiosity. The Civil War was fought during this era, and after the war the South needed to be reconstructed. The demand for goods and materials was tremendous. Inventors developed machines to make or provide the materials needed for the new construction. Railroads could ship this material almost anywhere. Due to the machine, the marketplace was able to provide for people's desire for things unique and exotic. Architecture responded with many new styles. This section will focus on several, and there are others to investigate that may appeal to you.

GOTHIC REVIVAL, CIRCA 1840–1880 (FIGURE 4-11)

Borrowed from the Medieval Age when castles, turrets, tall arched windows, and decorative carved woodwork were used in buildings, this style favors craftsmanship, a return to handmade as opposed to machine-made items. Steeply pointed roof lines characterize the style. Gingerbread carvings usually hang from the eaves or front porches. It typically has bay windows and dormers with pointed or arched windows. It was constructed with vertical board and batten wood siding.

What are bay windows? What are dormers? Where are they located in this house? What purpose does each serve? What noteworthy American architect was influential in promoting this style? Locate a picture of a famous painting by Grant Wood that features a gothic revival farm house. What elements do you see in that house that are evident in the figure as well? What purposes do those elements serve?

ITALIANATE, CIRCA 1840–1885 (FIGURES 4-2, 4-3, AND 4-4)

You were introduced to this style in the beginning of this unit. The style reflects the Romantic notion of faraway places that Americans of this era viewed as peaceful and contemplative, with a sense of tradition. Gardens were a part of the Italianate plan.

What is a villa? Why were villas usually two or more stories high? Why would Americans be interested in a style that represented a sense of tradition? What elements do you note in the building? What purposes do they serve?

SECOND EMPIRE, CIRCA 1855–1885 (FIGURE 4-12)

Influenced by the Second Empire reign of Napoleon III of France (1852–1870), this style was considered very modern in its day. The style has a mansard roof, which is boxy, slanted at various angles, and shaped to provide living spaces in the attic. The varied angles and pitch of the roof are sometimes straight, straight with a slight outward flair, concave or convex. The dormer windows, usually decorative in nature, have rounded tops. The style also has pediment tops or double windows.

Who was François Mansard? Why is this style of roof known by his name? How do these dormer windows compare to the ones in figure 4-11? What characteristics do you note about this style? What purposes do they serve?

STICK STYLE, CIRCA 1860–1890 (FIGURE 4-13)

In this style, wood siding is cut and arranged within borders so the focus is on wooden surface textures and patterns. Sections of flat boards are placed in various patterns on the outer side walls of the house for the same reason. Textures and patterns could be rough, curved, or triangular, and could be used in shingles or siding. Light creates strong contrasts on the surfaces of the siding, making textures and shapes more evident and interesting.

Notice how the placement of the siding creates interesting patterns, especially under the eaves of the right side of the house. Why would a designer use this stick style? What other characteristics do you see incorporated into this style? What purposes do they serve? What similarities do you see to Gothic revival style? How does the use of chimneys compare to the use of chimneys in other styles?

QUEEN ANNE, CIRCA *1880–1910* (FIGURE *4-14*)

This style of architecture was very popular in America after the 1876 Philadelphia Centennial Exposition. Its eclectic style incorporates classical, romantic, and exotic shapes. It is usually asymmetrical, with towers, turrets, wraparound porches, and many types of windows and doors. The wooden spindle work and brackets are used under porches and roof eaves.

What was the Philadelphia Centennial Exposition? Why was this architectural style called Queen Anne? What features can you identify? What purposes did they serve? What was going on in the United States at the time? How did this event affect the various materials and the hardware use in the construction of this building? Speculate on the reasons the houses are so big.

TURN OF THE NINETEENTH CENTURY

It was the time of the Industrial Revolution and America was prospering. Many people left rural areas to find work in the city. Factories were built all over the country, providing work for many, including thousands of new immigrants coming to our shores. The machine age was in full speed. Transportation improved; trains, street cars, and automobiles began to have an impact on where people worked and lived. The middle class wanted and bought wares produced in this age. There were also rich industrialists who built huge estates in styles borrowed from Europe. There was a renewed interest in things American due to the celebration of the country's centennial. Styles such as colonial and federal were revived and became fashionable again. Henry Hobson Richardson and Louis Sullivan, two great American architects, were attempted to find a fresh approach to architecture through innovations.

SHINGLE STYLE, CIRCA *1880–1900*

This one you will have to research on your own! This style was usually used in vacation homes. The outer surface of the building was covered completely in wooden shingles. They were built to accommodate an informal lifestyle. Interesting features were added to these buildings.

> Where are these types of buildings usually located? Why are they covered with wooden shingles? Why did they fall out of popularity quickly?

RICHARDSONIAN, CIRCA *1880–1900* (FIGURE 4-15)

 Inspired by Romanesque models found in Europe, this style was named for the Boston architect Henry Hobson Richardson (1838–1886). It is a heavy-looking style, with a massive, even fortresslike appearance. It was built of rough-cut stone and brick. Images of plant and animal forms were carved into the capitals and bases of the arch supports or columns. Towers, turrets, and rounded side ends also characterized this style. It was an expensive style to build even then.

> What was the Romanesque period? What is a capital? Why is the building in the figure called a *cushion capital*? Why was this type of architecture expensive to build? What unique features do you notice? What purposes do they serve?

THE REVIVALS

Revival means "a coming back into use; a new life or consciousness." At the turn of the twentieth century and through the years of World War I and World War II right up through the 1950s, America wanted to return to architectural styles that recalled earlier times. These styles were drawn from American and European styles such as American colonial, Tudor English, French château, Spanish mission, and German or Swiss chalet. A Pueblo revival occurred in the Southwest.

COLONIAL REVIVAL, CIRCA 1900 (FIGURE 4-16A)

Based on Georgian or federal architectural styles from the second half of the eighteenth century or first part of the nineteenth century, American colonial is the most popular revival style built around 1900. Georgian, federal, and Dutch gambrel styles exist all over the United States. The style is very similar to the eighteenth-century colonial houses, with the addition of garages and open-sided or screened porches. It is also characterized by double sets of windows. Classical details mark the entrances.

Why were the original styles called colonials? What similarities do you see between figure 4-16a and the original colonial styles? What features are added in the revival example? What purposes do they serve?

NEOCLASSICAL REVIVAL, CIRCA 1893 (FIGURE 4-16B)

Revived at the 1893 World's Columbian Exposition in Chicago, this style's scale and classical details are evident in the figure. The use of columns in the front of the structures reflects the classical theme. The columns are usually two full stories tall. They support the gables of the front porch or entrance. The look is very formal and symmetrical.

What event is taking place in the figure? Why was this style selected for this particular event? What is a *peristyle*? How is it evident in this building? What other revival styles used columns? What other features do you notice? What purposes do they serve?

TUDOR REVIVAL, CIRCA 1920S AND 1930S (FIGURE 4-16C)

In the 1920s and 1930s, Americans became fascinated with the country or cottage lifestyle of fifteenth-century Tudor England. The style was used in simple cottages as well as in the grand houses of wealthy industrialists. The building materials were stone, brick, wood, and leaded glass. The steeply pitched roofs were made of asphalt shingles and gables of various sizes instead of thatch. The chimneys were built of patterned brick or decorated stone-work. Chimney pots were placed on top of chimney openings. Oriel windows, a combination of bay window and leaded glass, were commonly used. Cut stonework was often used around the front door. Although always asymmetrical, the style was built with one-, two-, and three-story sections to create interesting combinations of forms.

> Who were the Tudors? What was the purpose of chimney pots? What is leaded glass? Where have you seen homes of this style in your community? Note some of the features of this example. What purposes do they serve?

CHATEAU REVIVAL, CIRCA 1895 (FIGURE 4-16D)

Based on the château styles of France in the 1500s and 1600s, this style is used for public buildings as well as for mansions of the wealthy. This style is expensive to build and therefore seldom used. Richard Morris Hunt, who designed Biltmore, a mansion built in 1895 in North Carolina for George W. Vanderbilt, popularized it in America. It has Gothic and Renaissance details, including rounded turrets and dormer windows with pointed finials on each side. Details are carved around the windows and doors. The roof is steeply pitched, usually in the hipped style. The building exteriors are made of stone, stucco, or brick, painted a light color. There are usually three or more massive stone chimneys.

> What is a château? Who was George W. Vanderbilt? Find his home in a book or on the Internet. What features do you see in his home and the one in the figure? What purposes do the features serve?

BEAUX-ARTS REVIVAL (FIGURE 4-16E)

The French term meaning "fine arts" refers to a style revived in America by architects who studied at the Ecole des Beaux-Arts, a famous art school in Paris. It was copied extensively by Americans. It has a very formal look, with large stone pillars and wall surfaces that are decorated with carved stone garlands. The exteriors are usually stone, with the flat surface cut into rectangles. The buildings are always symmetrical. The roof line sometimes has a stone balustrade as well as stone quoins. It has a number of massive windows, often half rounded at the top to let light into the rooms. The windows often have French doors that lead to a terrace. Formal gardens or formal landscaped plazas lead pedestrians into the space.

> How is the French term for this style pronounced? What is a balustrade? What are quoins? What purposes do they serve? What other elements do you see? What purposes do they serve?

ITALIANATE RENAISSANCE REVIVAL, CIRCA *1890* THROUGH *1930* (FIGURE 4-16F)

Influenced by the design of the Vatican (begun in 1506 by Donato Brante and later finished by Michelangelo), the Uffizi Gallery (designed by Giorgio Vasari in 1560 to 1580), and other architecture of the Italian Renaissance, this style was brought to America by architects and architectural firms who studied in Europe in the late nineteenth century. One such architectural firm was the famous McKim, Mead, and White. The style was used for homes and public buildings such as libraries, art museums, and universities. It is a very sophisticated style, solid-looking and impersonal. Smooth or rough-cut stone is used for the exterior, with brick and stone quoins on the outside. The roof is usually hipped. Brackets are sometimes placed under the eaves or overhang. A stone parapet that runs around the entire building hides the roof line. The recessed porch or entryway is usually symmetrical, with the door placed in the center and flanked by a series of large windows.

> What is the Vatican? Where is it located? What is a parapet? What are some of its other famous architectural and design features? What purposes do they serve?

MISSION AND SPANISH ECLECTIC REVIVAL, CIRCA *1920* THROUGH *1930* (FIGURE 4-16G)

Designed in the Spanish architectural style found in Mexico and Latin America, this style was introduced at the Panama-California Exposition in San Diego in 1915. It was a hit with other architects and designers and was especially popular in warmer climates. Although found all over the United States, it died out in the 1940s. It is characterized by one or two stories. It has low-pitched roofs, sometimes hipped and gabled, covered with red or green tiles. Arched doorways have carved wood front doors and surrounds carved in stone or wood. The elaborate iron grills cover the entrance or windows and are used as gates to garden entrances. The style has a stucco or brick exterior. Fancy chimney tops are added for decoration. It has an informal, comfortable asymmetrical plan and overall look. The interior or rear gardens often have a water feature such as a fountain.

> Why did this style have tiled roofs? Why were these houses covered with stucco or brick? What might be some reasons for the iron grill gates and doorways? What other elements do you notice? What purposes do they serve?

DESIGNS OF THE TWENTIETH CENTURY

New styles of architecture that broke from tradition were birthed in the twentieth century. The work of Frank Lloyd Wright, one of the more famous architects, challenged the prevailing ideas about architectural style. Craftsmanship (handmade products) and modern (machine-made) styles each had their supporters and critics. Architects fleeing Germany before World War II brought contemporary approaches to the United States. The postmodern style also had an impact on contemporary architecture.

PRAIRIE STYLE, CIRCA 1900–1920 (FIGURE 4-17)

Truly an American form of architecture, this style was made popular by Frank Lloyd Wright, who believed that architecture should complement the landscape and become part of it. The style began in Chicago, where Wright established his own school to train architects in his beliefs and approaches. It became popular throughout the country. Characterized by an emphasis on the horizontal, it has long, wide lines. The low-hipped roofs project beyond the end walls. Rows of identical windows wrap around corners. Broad flat chimneys rise above the roof line. Arched entrances are placed off center.

> What exterior materials did Frank Lloyd Wright use? How were his interiors different from those of previous styles? What other innovations did he develop? What purposes did they serve? How long was his style popular in the United States?

CRAFTSMAN, CIRCA *1905–1930* (FIGURE *4-18*)

Sparked by a late nineteenth-century artistic movement in England, this style turned away from the machine-age elements to return to the human need to create. Builders used simple hand tools and basic materials to create functional buildings and furniture that reflect craftsmanship. A very popular style all over the United States, examples are found in every community. It was sometimes called *bungalow*. A full-width front porch characterizes it. The low-pitched, gabled roofs have overhangs and brackets. It is constructed of wood siding, with a stone or brick fireplace. The sideboards are built in, with glass doors.

> What famous architects and designers are associated with this style? What is a sideboard? What purpose does it serve? How does the Craftsman house compare to other styles in terms of appearance, cost, and functionality for the working family?

ART MODERNE STYLE, CIRCA *1925–1980* (FIGURE *4-19*)

The art moderne style used streamlined industrial designs drawn from ship and automobile construction. It was used in movie theaters, diners, skyscrapers, offices, and homes. The style emphasizes horizontal lines. It has curved corners, glass block windows, and window walls. Stepladder elements are made from pipe material used in ship construction. It is a clean and sleek design.

> In what ways was architecture affected by the industrial design used in means of transportation? Locate buildings of this style in your community. What other elements do you notice? What purposes do they serve?

INTERNATIONAL STYLE, CIRCA *1925–1980* (FIGURE *4-20*)

Transplanted by architects and designers who escaped from Europe during World War II, this style drew upon the integration of science and industry, and upon creativity and expression. The style had the motto "Say more with less." Leading architects were Mies van der Rohe, Le Corbusier, Walter Gropius, and Philip Johnson. This style combined humanmade materials (steel, glass, plastics, laminates, chrome) with natural materials (wood, stone, and marble).

Architects used the machine and the latest in technology to create functional art as well as decorative art. It has a sleek, clean look, perfect for skyscrapers. This style is found mainly in large urban centers, but sometimes it is used for homes in smaller communities. The idea is that the home is a machine for living; there are few ornaments or decorative spaces that do not contribute to the needs of the family.

> What does "say more with less" mean? What are the principal structural elements in the buildings in the figure? What purposes do they serve? What is its sheeting or outer covering? How did the architect create the curve in the tallest building?

POSTMODERN, CIRCA *1970*–PRESENT (FIGURE *4-21*)

This style rejected the "say more with less" concept. It used architectural styles of the past as a visual allegory, telling stories about those architectural styles. The classical elements, including columns, pediments, and Palladian-styled windows, were symmetrically arranged. The result was a heavy overall look. Builders used a variety of materials. The style was usually used in commercial or public buildings, and occasionally for homes.

> What does the term *postmodern* mean? What is a visual allegory or metaphor? What postmodern buildings are in your community? What elements do you find most fascinating? What purposes do those elements serve?

CONSTRUCTION

MORE ARCHITECTURAL ADVENTURES

CONSTRUCTION

MORE ARCHITECTURAL ADVENTURES

 ### 4-1: CARVING A STYLE IN TIME

To begin your exploration into styles of American architecture, create your own model of a building:

Step 1. Use a large, fresh bar of soft white soap, such as Ivory. Place the soap on a piece of paper and draw around it to outline its widest sides (which will be the front and back of your building) as well as the narrow sides (the sides of your building).

Step 2. In one large rectangle, draw the facade of a building that visually pleases you. You might include columns and decorative designs around the windows and roof, or perhaps you prefer a simpler design, with less embellishment. Show all six sides of the building, including the top and bottom. If the building is not large enough to suit you, draw pieces to extend it on the sides or back.

Step 3. Place your drawing on the soap. Trace over it with a sharp pencil to transfer the outlines to the soap.

Step 4. Using a blunt tool such as a kitchen knife or small tool for carving clay, carefully scrape and carve the surface of the soap, cutting away larger pieces not included in your design. For more decorative sections, use a finer, sharper point, such as an untwisted paper clip, a safety pin, or sharpened pencil. If you use a mat knife, be very careful of its sharp edge and point! To make an area more rounded, put a little water on your finger or a paper towel and smooth the edges.

Step 5. Place your building on a piece of cardboard or in a plastic box to protect it.

Step 6. Display your building in the classroom. As this unit continues, compare your building with the styles being described and take notes on any similarities you see between your building and those in the photographs. By the conclusion of the unit, you will be familiar with many styles and will be able to share your building with the class as an example of a particular style or combination of styles.

4-2: CHARTING THE STYLES

To help you see the differences between the styles presented in this unit, make a chart.

Step 1. Across the top of a large piece of paper or on a computer spreadsheet, as column headings write various elements you have seen in the in the descriptions of styles (roof types, window types, materials used, special features, and so on; see chart below).

Step 2. Down the left side of the chart, list the styles you have studied.

Step 3. Draw horizontal and vertical lines to finish your chart.

Step 4. Go back through the descriptions, writing the descriptive words in the appropriate boxes. Some will have more information than others; some might be blank; some may need an extra column, depending on the labels you wrote across the top.

Step 5. In this chart, identify the styles of buildings you see around your community.

	Date	Roof	Chimney	Windows	Materials
Post-Medieval English	1600–1700	steeply pitched	large, with stack	small with many panes	stone, brick, wood siding

4-3: APPLYING KNOWLEDGE OF STYLE

Many variations of each architectural style exist. Combinations of two styles are also common, especially during times of transition. It is also possible to find a building in one style with an addition in a later style. This exercise offers helpful steps to determine the architectural style of a building.

Step 1. Look at a building from various angles—front, both sides, and back. Note how all the parts are put together.

Step 2. Cut a 2-by-2-inch window in a 3-by-5-inch card. Look through the window at the building, moving the window around to capture the details of the building.

Step 3. Record in a notebook all the characteristics you see. You may want to use an architectural style guide as a reference (see bibliography). Sketch in the overall appearance as well as details that make the building unique. Take photographs, if possible.

Step 4. If you know the date and builder, record that information, too. If not, try to ascertain the name of the architect or builder by reading the earliest records you can find at the courthouse.

Step 5. Look at your soap model of a building. Use a smaller square in a smaller card to identify the elements and determine the style of your model.

Step 6 Share the two buildings—the photographs of the one in your community and your soap carving—with your class. Note the styles of the buildings and explain how you came to your conclusions.

4-4: TAKING AN ARCHITECTURAL INVENTORY OF YOUR TOWN

Now that you have some experience in determining style, take inventory with your classmates of the architectural styles in your community. Create a visual time line that includes many of the styles in this chapter.

Step 1. Divide into teams and decide whether each team will take one particular area of the city, one style from this unit, or one type of building (homes, schools, libraries, city halls, shopping malls, downtown areas, firehouses, courthouses, industrial buildings). The age and layout of your city may determine the best way to go.

Step 2. Take an inventory of buildings that clearly represent each specific architectural style. Use the cut-out window technique to isolate elements that will help you determine style.

Step 3. With a camcorder or camera, tape or photograph these examples, including the details (doors, windows, roofs, eaves, gables, chimneys) that identify it as such.

Step 4. Find deeds or plans in the county records department that give you additional information about your buildings. Or talk to local historians to determine dates of construction, including additions to your building. Prepare a time line that depicts the ages and examples of the styles starting with the earliest and continuing through to the most recent.

Include, when possible, architectural drawings or plans of the buildings and the classical or traditional elements used in your examples.

Step 5. Share this report with the rest of your class or other classes in the school; you might want to schedule your presentation to fall during National Historic Preservation Week, which occurs in May.

4-5: AMERICAN HISTORY AND ARCHITECTURAL STYLE: RESEARCHING CONNECTIONS

To see the larger picture of how architecture is influenced by history, select a period in American history up through the nineteenth century and research that era. Your classmates will investigate other eras. Research your era. Answer such questions in your research as the following:

- What were the political factors that influenced this period? Who was president during this time?
- What were the major events and key issues (war, epidemics, natural disasters)?
- What were the general cultural, commercial, and spiritual attitudes? Who were the key people who influenced American life during that time?
- What was life like for the average American citizen in the urban and rural parts of the country?
- What industrial, scientific, or technological discoveries or inventions were made or created?
- What forms of creative expression (art, music, dance, theater, literature) were popular? Who were the main artists, performers, writers, and other celebrities? What fashions were popular?
- What major cultural events (such as world fairs or major art exhibits) took place?
- What films, photographs, or works of art, created either during the time period or more recently, reflect the era?

Develop a multimedia presentation that highlights this period. Include a mural, diorama, photographs, drawings, collage, clothing, jewelry, other memorabilia, authentic music, or other artifacts. Lead your audience to experience this style from many artistic perspectives. Consider these ideas or develop some of your own:

- Record your presentation on videotape and include music, visual art, and architectural styles.

- Record music and prepare a large poster board to mount your visual aids.
- Write a skit that emphasizes the architectural style and related art forms of this time period. The main character will be a major American architect. Perform your skit.

4-6: WHAT WAS IN STYLE: RESEARCHING TWENTIETH-CENTURY FASHIONS AND TASTE

Music, cars, buildings, dances, clothes, jewelry, and hairstyles are just a few examples of items that reflect fashion. Fashion changes from year to year, decade to decade, place to place. Choose one decade in the twentieth century, making sure you and your classmates each choose a different one. Study the changing fashions in that decade.

Step 1. Research the fashion of the decade you have chosen: cars, clothing, music, dance, records or tapes, film or other dramatic works, and so on. Analyze anything that influenced the way people looked, thought, behaved, or were entertained. If your decade happens to be one in which your grandparent or other relatives lived, you might have primary (firsthand) sources of information. Otherwise, use the library, Internet, or other secondary sources you have already discovered in this architectural journey.

Step 2. Locate examples of architecture and interiors. Review the major historical events of your decade and consider how the fashions of the time reflected or were related to these events.

Step 3. Prepare a creative multimedia report and present it in a style that presents various fashions of the day. Include visual aids, music, examples of clothing, dances, newspaper clippings, advertisements, movies, or TV shows that reflect the fashions and tastes of the time. Consider staging a debate, contest, or a TV news show as your mode of presentation, or use one of the suggestions from the previous activity.

4-7: ARCHITECTURE FOR CUSTOMS AND TRADITIONS

Every group of people in the history of America took time out from their busy schedules to celebrate life. These celebrations were unique to the community and took place at different times throughout the year. Some celebrations were seasonal, some religious, others patriotic, and others were associated with cultural traditions.

Step 1. Take a period of time associated with a specific architectural style we have studied. Given what you have learned about that era, make some predictions about the kinds of celebrations the people may have held and the manner in which they may have conducted these celebrations. Write your predictions and the reasoning behind them.

Step 2. Now research the celebrations that were held during that time, including the buildings that were used to house the celebrations.

Step 3. Compare your predictions with the information you discover in your research. Make a chart or graph showing the results and present it to your class.

4-8: FACT-FINDING SYMPOSIUM: THE GREAT AMERICAN ARCHITECTS AND DESIGNERS

Some styles of American architecture are associated with various celebrated architects who in some way contributed to the styles we find in our human-made landscape.

Step 1. Select an architect from the list or choose one from your research. (Do not choose Frank O. Gehry or Robert A.M. Stern; you will study them later.) No more than two students should study the same architect. Use a variety of sources to research your architect's life and ideas on architecture and building techniques.

Step 2. Analyze the work of this architect—the cultural influences on his or her style, the ways in which the style is similar to or different from the pure styles we have studied, his or her beliefs and values as reflected in the building, and so on. Evaluate the work of your architect as it, in turn, influenced culture.

Step 3. Now have some creative fun with your research. The class will vote on a building that the community needs (for example, a new theater, housing development, city government complex, parks and recreation facility). Plan and put on an architectural symposium in your class or for other classes. You will become your architect, perhaps even dressing like he or she would, and pitch a marketing plan that explains why you should be hired to design the project. If you work in pairs to do your research, one of you can play the role of the architect and the other can be an assistant in the firm. Review your personal history and how you developed your beliefs about architecture. Describe the buildings you designed and the materials you used in your projects. Include photographs or models of buildings in the style of your architect.

Step 4. During the symposium, the audience (community members represented by your classmates or others) will fill out an evaluation form that lists considerations in the hiring process: style of the architect, purpose of the building, appropriateness of the architect's proposal to the needs of the project, history of the architect. For each presentation, the audience will score the architect according to the needs of the project.

Step 5. At the conclusion of the symposium, collect and tabulate the evaluations to determine which architect to hire for the project.

Thomas Jefferson	François Mansard
Asher Benjamin	Henry Hobson Richardson
Robert Adam	Richard Norman Shaw
Minard Lafever	Richard Morris Hunt
Chistopher Wren	McKim, Mead, and White
William Strickland	Louis Sullivan
Inigo Jones	Mary Jane Coulter
Thomas U. Walter	Frank Lloyd Wright
James Gibbs	Walter Burley Griffin
Alexander Jackson Davis	Cass Gilbert
William Jay	Henry Mather Green
Andrea Palladio	Charles Sumner Green
Benjamin Latrobe	Eliel Saarinen
John Haviland	Gustav Stickley
Robert Mills	Walter Gropius
Alexander Parris	Maya Lin
Andrew Jackson Downing	Robert Venturi
Isaiah Rodgers	Mies van der Rohe
William Thornton	Charles Moore
Orson S. Fowler	Philip Johnson
Samuel McIntire	Eero Saarinen
Bernard Maybeck	Julia Morgan

Architecture Everywhere, © 2000 Zephyr Press, Tucson, Arizona

4-9: CREATING AN ARCHITECTURAL DESIGN FIRM

An architectural firm joins several architects, designers, draftsmen, interior designers, and others to attract clients. Members of the firm work as a team on projects. So far, you have worked individually and in various small groups. You are now going to become a member of a new architectural firm.

Step 1. A design firm must have architects with various viewpoints to meet the needs of a wide variety of clients. List three classmates with whom you think you can work well. They will not necessarily be your friends, but classmates who have ideas very different from yours. Your goal is to include a variety of strengths and attitudes. Give your list to me, and I will place you with at least one of your preferred partners, while creating a balance in each four- to five-member team.

Step 2. Meet with your new architectural design team. Share your favorite activities in this architecture course. From this discussion, you may find that some members are good at two-dimensional drawings, while others like doing models. Some may prefer the writing assignments, and others have enjoyed doing presentations. Look for at least one attribute that each team member brings to your new architectural firm.

Step 3. Decide who will play what role (president, architect, interior designer, and so on) in your firm.

Step 4. A business needs a name. With your group, decide on an appropriate name for your architectural firm. It might incorporate all of your last names or your initials, or perhaps it will reflect some architectural strength or value your group shares. To get some additional ideas, look in the telephone directory or in professional architectural magazines to see what some others have chosen.

Step 5. Design a logo for your company to include on the firm's stationery and business cards, in advertisements, and on the sign for your building. With your firm members, brainstorm some ideas; accept all suggestions as they arise and record them on a chart. Each person will take one idea and develop a design that in some way reflects the firm's name and the mission. Meet again and review the designs. You may all agree on one, or perhaps create a new one by combining elements of several. Your team may even decide to change its name to go with a design that everyone likes.

Step 6. Create business cards for each member of the firm. Every card will have the same design: the person's name and position, the firm's name and logo, the address and phone number of your school. Check out some actual business cards in a stationery store order book for ideas.

Step 7. Introduce your architectural firm to the class, explaining the philosophy of your company as it is reflected in the design of your card.

Your architectural firm will be your working team for the remainder of team activities. Occasionally people do change employment, so if a problem arises with your team, discuss it with your teacher, who will help decide if a change is necessary.

4-10: COMFORT AND FASHIONS: RESEARCHING INTERIORS

Over the centuries, people have attempted to design or decorate the inside rooms of their homes with an emphasis on function and comfort, while still making the rooms attractive and pleasing. People are interested in how furniture, draperies, wall coverings, flooring, and objects on walls or on furniture can enhance the ambience of a building.

Step 1. Choose either two different architectural styles several years apart or one type of room in a house (kitchen, living room, bedroom).

Step 2. Research how interior decorative elements contributed to the ambience of buildings designed in the styles you have chosen. If you have chosen a room, research how that room was decorated at various times. Use the library, Internet, old decorating magazines, period rooms in art museums, or historic house museums.

Step 3. Compare and contrast your findings, looking for changes over time. Speculate on the reasons for the changes.

Step 4. Present your information in a visual report. Bring in wall coverings, fabrics, floor samples, color charts, or furniture models to complement your report. Some paint stores or furniture stores might give you samples, and you might find furniture models in a toy store, hobby shop, or dollhouse store. If you prefer, you may construct a three-dimensional model of a particular interior room to illustrate your research.

Architecture Everywhere, © 2000 Zephyr Press, Tucson, Arizona

4-11: Creating in Miniature

Miniatures are a popular hobby for many people. Miniatures are exteriors or interiors of buildings made to resemble, reproduce, or depict a style of architecture found in a particular area, a famous building, or an adaptation of a given style. Ancient civilizations, European royal families, American presidents, movie stars, and ordinary families all have had doll-houses and playhouses to provide youngsters with a place to play make-believe.

Step 1. Decide whether each architectural firm will work on dollhouse construction using one of the different styles presented in this unit, or if the class will work on one house together, with one style being chosen and each firm taking a room.

Step 2. As a team, construct a miniature dollhouse or playhouse. Use either a kit from a hobby shop or miniature store, or build your own model. If you build one, first draw the plans and decide on a scale, such as 1 inch equals 1 foot. Be sure that everyone's buildings are based on this scale. Dollhouses usually have an open back side or a front that opens on hinges to allow furniture and small toys to be moved around inside.

Step 3. Use the architectural colors and the type of detailing appropriate for your style of house. Glue scraps of paper on the walls, put coverings on the floors, and make cloth or paper curtains and rugs. Find or construct the appropriate furniture, as well as wall hangings and other decorative items for the style and era of the house.

Step 4. After the house is complete, take it to a preschool or kindergarten class and observe or photograph the children's reactions to your project. You will see why miniature houses have been popular for centuries! You may want to donate the dollhouse to a preschool or the PTA for a fund-raiser, or give it to a community agency as a gift for a needy family at holiday time.

4-12: Architectural Styles in Wood and Clay Relief

Instead of a dollhouse, use wood or clay to construct just the front facade of a building. In artistic terms, *relief* means "adding layered details to a flat base." When complete, mount the wood or clay facades on backings you can hang on the wall of the classroom.

Wood

Step 1. Use thin pieces of wood you can cut easily with sharp scissors or a small saw. Wood supplies can be found at a hobby or miniature store.

Step 2. Make a scale drawing of the facade of the house. Cut out the outline and transfer it to a piece of wood by placing a piece of carbon paper under the drawing and tracing over it with a pencil.

Step 3. Cut the outside lines on the wood to outline the facade.

Step 4. Draw and cut out the roof and glue it to the background. Continue the process of adding detailed pieces to your facade (window surrounds, columns, sconces).

Step 5. Paint the wood and coat it with a polymer finish.

Clay

Step 1. Use self-hardening clay. With a rolling pin or rounded dowel, roll out a clay slab about ½-inch thick. Draw the outline of your facade on paper and transfer to the clay by tracing it with a sharp pencil.

Step 3. Use a clay tool or kitchen knife to cut out the facade.

Step 4. Draw and cut out the roof and other details. To bind two pieces of clay, use a sharp tool to scratch marks onto the surfaces to be joined. Mix equal parts of water and clay to form a paste called *slip*. Brush the slip between the clay pieces and press in place.

Step 5. After the clay dries, paint the facade and coat with polymer.

     Architecture Everywhere, © 2000 Zephyr Press, Tucson, Arizona

Unit 4
Photos

▲ *FIGURE 4-1. WILLIAM THORNTON'S CAPITOL BUILDING WAS STARTED IN 1793 AND FINISHED IN 1830. BENJAMIN HENRY LATROBE AND CHARLES BULFINCH WERE OTHER ARCHITECTS WHO WORKED ON THE BUILDING AFTER THORNTON. (PHOTO COURTESY OF HABS)*

◄ *FIGURE 4-2. THE MORRIS-LIBBY HOUSE IN PORTLAND, MAINE, IS AN EXAMPLE OF THE ITALIANATE STYLE. THIS STYLE USUALLY HAS A TALL TOWER AND LARGE BRACKETS UNDER THE EAVES OR OVERHANG OF THE ROOF. IT ALSO USES SUCH CLASSICAL DETAILS AS PILLARS OR PEDIMENTS OVER WINDOWS AND DOORS, AND STONE OR BRICK SHAPES AT THE CORNERS CALLED QUOINS. (PHOTO COURTESY OF HABS)*

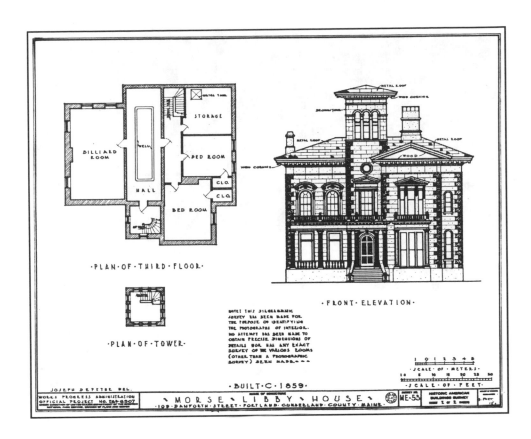

▶ FIGURE 4-3. BASED ON
WHAT YOU SEE ON THE
THIRD FLOOR, WHAT
ROOMS WOULD YOU FIND
ON THE FIRST AND
SECOND FLOORS?
(PHOTO COURTESY OF
HABS)

▶ FIGURE 4-4. THE HENRY SHAW HOUSE IN
ST. LOUIS WAS BUILT IN 1849. COMPARE
AND CONTRAST THE ARCHITECTURAL
ELEMENTS FOUND IN FIGURES 4-2 AND 4-4.

FIGURE 4-5. THE PARSON CAPEN HOUSE (1683) IN TOPSFIELD, MASSACHUSETTS, IS A BEAUTIFUL EXAMPLE OF POST-MEDIEVAL ENGLISH STYLE USING WOOD. IMMIGRANTS FROM ESSEX AND KENT IN SOUTHEASTERN ENGLAND BUILT IT. (PHOTO BY E. KIDDER SMITH)

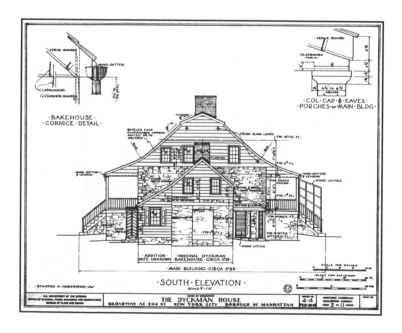

FIGURE 4-6. THIS DUTCH COLONIAL-STYLE HOME BUILT IN 1783 IS IN NEW YORK CITY. NOTICE THE GAMBREL ROOF WITH ITS SLOPING LINE. (PHOTO COURTESY OF HABS)

FIGURE 4-7. THIS HOUSE IS THE DYCKMAN HOUSE. DYCKMAN SETTLED IN NEW YORK, AS DID MANY OTHER DUTCH IMMIGRANTS. WHERE IS A DUTCH DOOR IN THIS DRAWING? (PHOTO COURTESY OF HABS)

Architecture Everywhere, © 2000 Zephyr Press, Tucson, Arizona

▶ FIGURE 4-8. THIS GRAND HOUSE IN THE GEORGIAN STYLE IS NEAR SHIRLEY, VIRGINIA. THE HOUSE WAS BUILT IN 1740 AND IS CALLED SHIRLEY PLANTATION. NOTICE THE SYMMETRICAL BALANCE; EVEN NUMBERS OF DOORS AND WINDOWS ARE PLACED ON EACH SIDE OF THE FRONT DOOR. (PHOTO COURTESY OF HABS)

▶ FIGURE 4-9. THE READ HOUSE IS A FINE EXAMPLE OF FEDERAL ARCHITECTURE. IT WAS BUILT IN 1801 IN NEW CASTLE, DELAWARE. COMPARE AND CONTRAST THE HOUSE WITH ONE IN THE GEORGIAN STYLE. LOOK CLOSELY! (PHOTO COURTESY OF HABS)

▶ FIGURE 4-10. THE CURTIS LEE HOME IN ARLINGTON, VIRGINIA, WAS BUILT IN 1820 IN A GREEK REVIVAL STYLE. IT IS THE ANCESTRAL HOME OF ROBERT E. LEE. IT IS ON THE GROUNDS OF ARLINGTON NATIONAL CEMETERY. DESCRIBE THE TEMPLE FORMS YOU SEE. (PHOTO COURTESY OF HABS)

▲ FIGURE 4-11. THIS HOUSE IS A SMALL GOTHIC REVIVAL HOME WITH A
STEEPLY PITCHED ROOF AND POINTED, ARCHED WINDOWS.

◀ FIGURE 4-12. IN SECOND EMPIRE STYLE
BUILDINGS SUCH AS THIS ONE, ADDITIONAL
ROOMS COULD BE BUILT INTO THE ATTIC SPACE
BECAUSE OF THE MANSARD ROOF DESIGN.
WHAT OTHER ELEMENTS DO YOU SEE?

▶ *FIGURE 4-13. THE EMLEN PHYSICK HOUSE IN CAPE MAY, NEW JERSEY, IS AN EXAMPLE OF THE STICK STYLE OF ARCHITECTURE. (PHOTO COURTESY OF HABS)*

◀ *FIGURE 4-14. TOWERS, TURRETS, BAY WINDOWS, AND WRAPAROUND PORCHES WERE POPULAR ELEMENTS OF THE QUEEN ANNE STYLE. DO YOU HAVE ANY QUEEN ANNE HOMES IN YOUR COMMUNITY?*

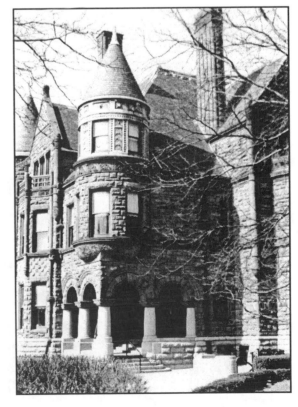

▶ *FIGURE 4-15. THIS PHOTOGRAPHS SHOWS AN EXAMPLE OF A ROUNDED COLUMN THAT SUPPORTS THE ARCH WITH A SQUARE, DECORATED CAPITAL CALLED A CUSHION CAPITAL. IT IS USUALLY CARVED WITH PLANT FORMS. NOTICE THE ROUGH-CUT STONE. THE HOUSE IS BUILT IN RICHARDSONIAN STYLE.*

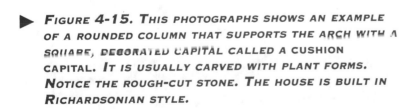

FIGURE 4-16A. THIS TURN-OF-THE-CENTURY HOUSE HAS A CLASSICAL FRONT ENTRANCE. IT WAS BUILT IN THE COLONIAL REVIVAL STYLE OF THE EIGHTEENTH CENTURY.

FIGURE 4-16B. THIS PHOTOGRAPH IS OF THE WEST VIEW OF THE PERISTYLE AT THE COLOMBIAN EXPOSITION HELD IN CHICAGO, ILLINOIS, IN 1893. (PHOTO COURTESY OF THE CHICAGO HISTORICAL SOCIETY)

◀ *FIGURE 4-16D. THIS HOUSE WAS DESIGNED WITH MANY ELEMENTS BORROWED FROM THE CHATEAUX OF FRANCE. WHAT CHARACTERISTICS DO YOU SEE?*

◀ *FIGURE 4-16E. THE BEAUX-ARTS STYLE WAS FORMAL AND SYMMETRICAL. NOTICE THE CARVED STONE BALUSTRADE OR RAILING AT THE TOP OF THE ROOF LINE.*

◀ *FIGURE 4-16F. THE RECESSED ENTRANCE, ARCHED FRONTS, AND HIPPED ROOFS WERE USED IN ITALIANATE RENAISSANCE REVIVAL ARCHITECTURE.*

◀ *FIGURE 4-16G. THE ELABORATE FRONT ENTRANCE, STUCCO-COVERED EXTERIORS, AND RED OR GREEN TILED ROOFS WERE USED IN THE MISSION AND SPANISH ECLECTIC STYLES.*

▶ *FIGURE 4-17. THE PRAIRIE STYLE ROBIE HOUSE IN CHICAGO, ILLINOIS, WAS DESIGNED BY FRANK LLOYD WRIGHT AND EMPHASIZED LONG HORIZONTAL LINES. (PHOTO COURTESY OF HABS)*

▶ *FIGURE 4-18. LOW-PITCHED, GABLED ROOFS AND FRONT PORCHES COVERING THE ENTIRE FRONT OF THE HOUSE WERE ELEMENTS IN THE CRAFTSMAN STYLE.*

▶ *FIGURE 4-19. GLASS BLOCK, SLEEK CURVED CORNERS, PLAIN WALL SURFACES, AND BOXY SHAPES WERE USED IN THE ART MODERNE STYLE.*

▲ *FIGURE 4-20. STEEL, GLASS, CHROME, AND NATURAL MATERIALS WERE USED IN THE INTERNATIONAL STYLE. TALL SKYSCRAPERS OFTEN USE THESE MATERIALS TO APPEAR CLEAN AND SLEEK.*

▲ *FIGURE 4-21. HERE IS A 1990S EXAMPLE OF A POSTMODERN BANK. NOTICE THE SYMMETRICAL BALANCE. WHAT TRADITIONAL ARCHITECTURAL ELEMENTS WERE USED?*

Unit 5

Every Person's Home Is a Castle

Be it ever so humble, there's no place like home.
—John Howard Payne

FOUNDATION

IN THIS UNIT, STUDENTS

■ TRACE THE CHANGES IN ARCHITECTURAL DESIGN OF U.S. HOMES FROM THOSE OF THE EARLY AMERICANS TO THE PRESENT.

■ LEARN THE STEPS IN BUILDING VARIOUS STYLES OF HISTORICAL HOMES.

■ PREDICT THE DESIGN OF HOMES OF THE FUTURE.

Photocopy the following and pass it out to students, read it aloud to them, or use your own way of getting the concepts across to them:

Two of basic human needs are to provide support and safe shelter for our families. Building a place to live and carry on the activities of family life has been a task of men and women for centuries. The shelter has evolved over time from simple dark caves to abodes made of natural materials to structures that reflect certain styles of architecture. The home has incorporated the needs and lifestyle of the family members who live there and reflects their aesthetic tastes through its construction, design, and decoration.

It is the dream of many American families to own their own homes. Through the years this dream has caused people to leave one country in search of a better way of life in a new one. Often while on this journey they were subjected to hardships, including hazardous terrain and unpredictable weather. In the early days of the United States, settlers tolerated these hardships to own the land, make a living from it, and build homes in which to raise their children.

RESOURCE SHELF

▶ photographs of houses from various periods of time

▶ books, magazines, and catalogs from previous decades

▶ books on the history of your community

▶ local libraries

▶ historical museums and societies

▶ relatives, builders, architects, and historic preservationists to interview

▶ historic homes

 Architecture Everywhere, © 2000 Zephyr Press, Tucson, Arizona

THE EVOLUTION OF THE AMERICAN HOME

DESIGN

MAIN IDEAS IN THIS SECTION

- We can trace the historical development of the American home from the seventeenth and eighteenth century right up through the twentieth century.
- Hard manual work was the key to survival in the early days of settlement, and everyone, including the children, played a role in building a home.
- Economic conditions, advancement of technology, and lifestyle have changed the ways homes are constructed.
- The home is designed for the needs of the family and those needs change from generation to generation.

MATERIALS

- ▶ figures 5-1 through 5-23e (see pages 149–158 for enlarged photos)

GUIDELINES FOR INSTRUCTION

In addition to photographs, this unit includes work sheets and drawings that depict particular types of homes and sometimes the methods of construction that were used. Definitions of the terms on the work sheets are in the glossary (page 206). Photocopy the drawings, worksheets, and glossary for your students.

For architectural adventure 5-4, students view a segment of the film *Witness*. The film is rated R and is not suitable for middle-school students. However, the scene depicts a community barn-raising that is appropriate for the unit. Cue the video to a place about 70 minutes into the 112 minute film, at the beginning of the scene in which the community is walking to the site to build the barn. Show the scene that begins before the midday meal and ends at sundown, when the walls of the barn are in place.

BLUEPRINTS
THE EVOLUTION OF THE AMERICAN HOME

Photocopy the following and pass it out to students or read it aloud to them.

We will probably all agree that our homes are very special and important to us. You have discovered that the homes of your grandparents and other relatives are also important. The home has been the center of American life for several hundred years, and it has evolved over the years, incorporating new features and additions that reflect the needs of the people throughout various periods. Historical events and trends, including the need for making good housing available to more people, have had a profound impact on the American home. We are going to examine several types of homes and methods of construction. We will also investigate how new inventions and technologies have changed the home. Then you will have the opportunity to design a home for the twenty-first century!

EARLY HOMES

Photocopy the following section for students to read or read it aloud to them. (Answers to the exercises are in the appendix, page 202.)

You are going to look at the earliest American homebuilders and the conditions and materials they used to create shelters. Look at the illustrations and then explore and research further.

POST-AND-BEAM

This type of construction for shelters was first used in Jamestown, Virginia, in 1607, and in Plymouth Plantation, Massachusetts, in 1627.

Investigate to learn more about this construction style.

Step 1. Define terms associated with post-and-beam building techniques: *thatch, clapboards, chimney, window frame, wooden planks, rafters, wall frame, wattle and daub, Y-shaped poles, woven sticks, timber frame, oil cloth, notched and pegged, mortise and tenon,* and *felling trees.*

Step 2. Look closely at figures 5-1 through 5-8 (enlarged figures are on page 149). Using your definitions, identify the drawing that best illustrates each element and building process. Think carefully because there are more definitions than there are pictures!

FIGURE 5-1

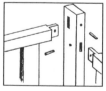
FIGURE 5-2

FIGURE 5-3

FIGURE 5-4

FIGURE 5-5

FIGURE 5-6

FIGURE 5-7

FIGURE 5-8

Figure 5-1.   _____

Figure 5-2.   _____

Figure 5-3.   _____

Figure 5-4.   _____

Figure 5-5.   _____

Figure 5-6.   _____

Figure 5-7.   _____

Figure 5-8.   _____

Step 3. Rearrange the figures in chronological order, starting with the first step in the construction process and ending with the last.

1. _____

2. _____

3. _____

4. _____

5. _____

6. _____

7. _____

8. _____

Step 4. Trade papers with someone in the class and compare your sequences. If they are different, discuss how each of you arrived at your conclusions. Then determine which sequence you both think is correct.

Step 5. Check your answers against those of your classmates.

THE LOG HOME

Many immigrants to the United States in the late eighteenth and early nineteenth centuries, especially those from Finland and Germany, used logs to build houses. Their method of construction was different from post-and-beam in that the size of the room was dependent on the length of the logs that they used for the four-sided "pen." The logs formed the outside and inside walls of the building. Log homes did not use wattle and daub. The logs were attached by notching the ends so they fit together snugly.

Here's your opportunity to become a log home builder, at least on paper!

Step 1. Figure 5-9 illustrates five different notching systems used in log construction. They are identified by capital letters *A* through *E*. Match the corresponding system with the appropriate drawing.

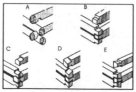

FIGURE 5-9

_____ Square notched

_____ V-notched

_____ Saddle notched

_____ Full dovetail

_____ Half dovetail

Step 2. Define these terms associated with this building technique: *chinking, adz, notching systems, wood shingles, rafters.*

Step 3. Research the steps or procedures used in log construction.

Step 4. Study figures 5-9A through 5-9E. Each illustration is labeled with capital letters *A* through *E*. They depict out-of-order steps in log home construction.

FIGURE 5-9A

FIGURE 5-9B

FIGURE 5-9C

FIGURE 5-9D

FIGURE 5-9E

Step 5. Organize figures 5-9A through 5-9E in the proper sequence of log home construction.

1. _____

2. _____

3. _____

4. _____

5. _____

Step 6. Compare your answers with those of your classmates, as in the last exercise.

FIGURE 5-10

FIGURE 5-10A

Figure 5-10 shows the location and home of a proud family. What famous American was born in a log home? Look at figure 5-10A for the answer. Where would you find log homes? How were they furnished on the inside? How and where did the settlers acquire their furnishings? If you have a log home in your community, take pictures or make a videotape for the class.

CONSTRUCTION
MORE ARCHITECTURAL ADVENTURES

5-1: Detective Work: Post-and-Beam vs Log Construction (page 139)

5-2: Life in a Log Home (page 139)

THE SOD HOUSE

As pioneers traveled westward to the plains of Kansas, Nebraska, the Dakotas, eastern Wyoming, Colorado, and Montana, they found few trees to build their homesteads. Being resourceful and in need of building materials, they used sod from the rich prairie. What is sod? The sod was cut with a special plow and then cut into large bricks and

FIGURE 5-11

stacked one on top of the other (see figure 5-11). These thick earthen walls provided good insulation in the winter and the summer. Sometimes the sod homes were built into the sides of hills.

The roof was the most difficult part to build. If there were trees around, they were cut and used for rafters, and then sod was laid on top. When money was available, the family bought wood shingles to cover the roof.

What major problems do you see with this type of construction? Why do you think there are few remaining examples of sod houses today? To understand the problems families encountered in constructing, caring for, and living in sod houses, read diaries and journals, or realistic fiction written by pioneers, especially by women, who generally cared for the homes. Many books in the bibliography outline this building process (Gintzler 1994, Greenwood 1994, Hechtlinger 1986, Wilder 1932, 1935).

CONSTRUCTION
MORE ARCHITECTURAL ADVENTURES

5-3: My Life as a Sod House (page 140)

EVOLVING TECHNOLOGY

Industrial innovations brought about many new methods of constructing homes. Life improved considerably as inhabitants became more comfortable in their homes.

BRICK CONSTRUCTION

In the nineteenth century, solid exterior brick walls began to be used. Unlike logs, sod, or wattle and daub, bricks were permanent, very strong, and required very little material to make. In the nineteenth century, solid exterior brick walls were used. Many walls were one foot thick and three stories tall. They were laid on foundations of stone or cement. Interior walls, too, were made of bricks.

FIGURE 5-12

Look at the home in figure 5-12, which was built in 1810. Why is the floor plan of the second floor in figure 5-12 identical to the first?

Immigrants brought brick making to America. Often the bricks were made on the grounds where the building was being constructed. Study figures 5-12A through 5-12D, which illustrate the steps that were used to make bricks in the nineteenth century. Brick masons used a variety of patterns to lay brick. These patterns were called *bonds*.

FIGURE 5-12A

FIGURE 5-12B

FIGURE 5-12C

FIGURE 5-12D

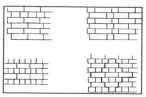

FIGURE 5-13

FIGURE 5-13A

Look at figure 5-13 (preceding page) and identify, from your research, common bond, Flemish bond, English bond, and Dutch cross bond. Give reasons for your guesses. Exchange answers with a classmate and justify your conclusions. Figure 5-13A (preceding page) shows a fine early brick home. What type of bond was used?

BALLOON AND STICK CONSTRUCTION, AND PATTERN BOOKS

FIGURE 5-14

Balloon frame construction was invented in Chicago and used around the 1830s. It drastically changed how homes were built, providing many more size and shape options. Speculate on the principles involved in the balloon method and reasons behind its name. Confirm your ideas by investigating how this method changed the construction of buildings forever. Stick construction is so named because individual pieces of lumber or sticks were used.

The practice of publishing pattern books or plan books began in the early nineteenth century. They were successful because they provided the middle class with an opportunity to build fine homes without having to hire an architect. People use pattern books today to select a type of home they may want to build. You can purchase them at supermarkets, drugstores, or convenience marts. If you like a particular design, you can order the plans and then get cost estimates from contractors. The books contain a wide variety of styles and plans to accommodate a variety of lifestyles.

Many famous architects in the nineteenth century made their patterns or plans available for mass publication. Figure 5-14 is a Bicknell design for a home in the 1870s. Bicknell would also custom design a house if someone desired.

To see how pattern books are used, follow these steps.

Step 1. Locate and study various pattern books or house plan books from various time periods. You can find them in libraries, used bookstores, or at garage or tag sales. Notice how housing fashions have changed over the years.

Step 2. Select a house plan from the past that you like.

Step 3. Write a paragraph or two stating your reasons for selecting that particular plan.

Step 4. Figure the 1890s cost of your house by multiplying the square feet by an average construction cost of $1.10 per foot.

THE MAIL-ORDER HOUSE

FIGURE 5-15

American industry was racing along in 1902. Manufactured goods of all kinds could be produced and shipped by train to warehouses or freight terminals all over the United States, Canada, and Mexico. Marketing and merchandising became an art, and the Sears and Roebuck catalog became the wish book of many Americans. An entire home could be built, decorated, furnished, and cleaned with products bought through this mail-order business.

Because of a strong job market and economy, more people could afford to build or buy homes, creating a higher demand for housing than ever before. For many the hand-me-downs of former generations became a thing of the past. American families prized new materials with which to build their homes. They enjoyed running water, electricity, indoor plumbing, ice boxes, and central heating systems.

For $1,700, a family could buy a new one-and-a-half story home (figure 5-15) from the Sears catalog. The building kit included everything, even the paint, door handles, and hardware. The materials for the house would arrive by rail, and the buyer or the Sears company would deliver the materials to the building site. For an additional fee, Sears would also erect the house on the lot.

Prefabricated homes (prefabs) were popular in the 1940s and 1950s. Lustron homes, made entirely of metal panels that were erected on the lot, were popular after World War II. There were other companies, too, that produced prefabs.

In a current Sears catalog or other catalog from a large mail-order company, identify ten items that are similar to those a family in the early 1900s would have found in their Sears catalog. Find twenty-five additional items that the same family would *not* have found in such a catalog. Compare your lists to those of your classmates.

CONSTRUCTION
MORE ARCHITECTURAL ADVENTURES

Architecture Everywhere, © 2000 Zephyr Press, Tucson, Arizona

CONTEMPORARY: 1940 TO PRESENT

After World War II, many GIs returned home to start families or raise those they left behind. The need for inexpensive housing was great, and attempts to design cheaper housing took several avenues.

The *Quonset hut,* a corrugated, half-rounded metal building, was used during World War II as a quick, inexpensive way to provide the military with offices, mess halls, barracks, and gymnasiums. Figure 5-16 shows an example. This type of housing was not generally used for domestic or family homes, but more for institutions.

FIGURE 5-16

Have you seen a Quonset hut in your area? If so, what is its current use?

The *mobile home* and mobile home parks were other American innovations during the 1940s and 1950s. Mobile homes were built at a factory and delivered with wheels so they could be moved from place to place as the family needed, or without wheels so they could be secured permanently onto a concrete pad in

FIGURE 5-17

a park. This type of construction provided the family with living, sleeping, eating, and bathroom facilities. The mobile home is usually less expensive than other types of homes. The interior of the mobile home is well designed, with an emphasis on getting the most out of the space. Some are quite elaborate and have many features found in traditional homes. Mobile homes and mobile home parks are home to thousands of Americans.

How has the mobile home in figure 5-17 been designed to look like a regular house? How has the surrounding area been designed to look like any yard?

FIGURE 5-18

The *A-frame* in figure 5-18 was also quite popular during the World War II era, especially for vacation homes. The A-frame is constructed so that the gabled roof serves as side walls as well. As with the Quonset hut, the roof continues to the ground and can be placed on top of basement walls. The interior allows for lofts or galleries and bedrooms on the upper level that open up to spaces below. The lower level contains living and dining areas as well as kitchens and bathrooms. The side walls are perfect for large windows, and patios or balconies are often attached. This style of home is inexpensive to build and allows for unconventional uses of space.

In what types of locations are most A-frame homes or buildings found today? What is their most common use?

FIGURE 5-19

The *geodesic dome* was the brainchild of Buckminster Fuller, a leading American architect, scientist, and philosopher during the 1960s and 1970s. He designed many buildings, including homes, using the principle of fitting together geometric shapes such as triangles. The triangles become polygrams, which Fuller assembled to create dome shapes that could serve many purposes. The polygrams were enclosed with thin pieces of steel, glass, wood, plastic, or fabric. The dome in figure 5-19 is covered with sheets of heavy plastic. His designs were innovative and practical to construct, and they allowed for maximum use of space.

For what purpose might a geodesic dome be used in an elementary school or park?

FIGURE 5-20

The *ranch-style home* (see figure 5-20) was also popular after World War II. In the 1940s and 1950s people became more dependent on their automobiles than on streetcars or bus systems. Therefore, new subdivisions built on the outskirts of the city often included attached garages. The exterior material of the homes was wood, brick, stone, or a combination. The homes were one-story structures, and the front usually stretched across the lot. The lots and yards were larger than those found in cities at the turn of the century. Rooms were often added to the front or rear of the main houses as the needs of the families changed.

What popular TV shows or movies that you have seen feature ranch-style houses?

Architecture Everywhere, © 2000 Zephyr Press, Tucson, Arizona

Another development was the *multilevel or split-level house*. This style used the basement and first story as living space. The entrance to the house split off; one could go up to the living room, kitchen, and bedrooms or down to the family or recreation room and additional bedrooms. The garage and utility room were also on the lower level. Sometimes there were three or four levels instead of two. Figure 5-21 shows a typical split-level house built in the 1980s.

FIGURE 5-21

FIGURE 5-22A

FIGURE 5-22B

All families did not live in single, detached homes built on lots with yards and trees. Many families lived in apartments, multiple homes with similar floor plans contained within a large exterior frame. Some were built with balconies, patios, terraces, fireplaces, garages, and greenhouses. Some, like the one in figure 5-22A, were several stories tall. There might be ten, twenty, or more apartments in one structure. When there are multiple buildings, it is called an *apartment complex*. Today there are many high-rise apartments that house urban families. Figure 5-22B is an example of such a building.

Builders use their creativity to construct apartment buildings of various materials.

> **BUILDING MATERIALS**
>
> BRICK
> WOOD
> TERRA COTTA
> STUCCO
> STONE
> GLASS
> STEEL

What are some advantages of living in a city apartment? List some conveniences. What are some disadvantages? What would it be like to live on the thirty-eighth floor of an apartment building? How would you get all your furniture into the apartment?

When someone owns an apartment, the apartment is called a *condominium*. In a condominium complex, owners take responsibility for managing their own units and the building as well. Usually, the owners form an association and set up rules and regulations to run and maintain the complex. A condominium looks similar to an apartment building and can have any number of floors, just as an apartment can.

If you live in a condominium, what rules do you have to follow? What rules don't you like to follow? If you don't live in one, what kinds of rules would you want the association to have to make life pleasant and safe for the residents? What rules would you feel were unjustified? Why?

FIGURE 5-22C

Today, as in the past, American families find themselves in various stages of transition. Often, due to circumstances beyond their control, they need a home for their families but can't afford one. These circumstances can lead to the need for housing assistance, which is often provided by charitable or religious groups and organizations such as Habitat for Humanity, or subsidized by state or federal governments. Sometimes the housing is a single home or an apartment such as the one in figure 5-22C. Others are in large complexes called *projects,* which are usually found in the city. Families generally pay rent based on their income. These units are basic, not lavish, but they provide for the needs of a family. Some of America's leading politicians, scientists, artists, writers, and businesspeople grew up in such housing complexes. Over the years, planners and architects have developed better designs and plans for building projects. The best examples are those that build in a sense of community.

CAUSES OF FINANCIAL HARDSHIP

JOB LOSS
DEATH OF A SPOUSE
DIVORCE
SINGLE-INCOME FAMILY
MEDICAL PROBLEMS

Find out about three or more well-known Americans who grew up in the projects. See if you can find an interview that asks them questions about the experience. What is a sense of community? Why would this contribute to the success of a housing project?

FIGURE 5-22D

Another popular housing type in some parts of the country today is the *patio home* (see figure 5-22D). This type of architecture is for the small family or busy professional who does not want to care for a large apartment or house. Patio homes are characterized by compact living areas. Each unit has a small, vest-pocket yard, and often incorporates a small patio off the living area. The complex is usually composed of many individual homes placed in asymmetrical units.

What types of housing other than those mentioned here are in your community? How are they similar to or different from those discussed here?

CONSTRUCTION
MORE ARCHITECTURAL ADVENTURES

HOMES OF THE FUTURE

How far apart are the houses in your neighborhood? Because of the scarcity of land, future houses may have as little as twelve feet between them. Architects will probably attempt to provide privacy through the design of the home. What do you think the home of the twenty-first century will be like? What unique features must they have for the families of the next century? Architect and designer Peter Eisenman, quoted by Jerry Adler (1990) in *Newsweek*, predicted that the house of the twenty-first century will still look like a house, "not a machine or a spaceship." It will not stand out as some weird structure. Figure 5-23A is an illustration of what such a house would look like from the front outside. In figure 5-23B you can see the rear, outside view of the house.

The lifestyles of the American family are predicted to be more informal; architects will respond by bringing interior partitions between rooms down. Inside, dining rooms, living rooms, kitchens, and dens will become one vast room for multifunctional family living and communication, as depicted in figure 5-23C. Look at the floor plans in figures 5-23D and 5-23E. These are the proposed living spaces for the family of the future. What new and innovative spaces, features, layouts, or room arrangements do you see here that we do not have in our homes today? What would you like and dislike about living in such a house?

FIGURE 5-23A

FIGURE 5-23B

FIGURE 5-23C

FIGURE 5-23D

FIGURE 5-23E

You will be spending your adult life in the twenty-first century. What will the family—your family—need to function in that century? Here is one way to plan for your future.

Step 1. Research life in the twenty-first century. Consider elements houses will need. Will recycling, passive solar heating, energy-efficient materials, gardens, aesthetic interiors, and exercise space be some of your considerations?

Step 2. List everything a family will need for a house.

Step 3. On graph paper or with a computer, map out a proposed floor plan for a future house.

Step 4. Draw the outside of your designed house, including front, back, and sides. Sketch two or more versions. Don't forget to include the type of materials you will use for the outside. If you agree that the homes of the future will look like a home and not a spaceship, will your design reflect any traditional elements, such as those found in the postmodern style? Or will you go for a futuristic appearance?

Step 5. Write a paragraph that discusses the positive and negative aspects of the floor plans you designed.

CONSTRUCTION
MORE ARCHITECTURAL ADVENTURES

          Architecture Everywhere, © 2000 Zephyr Press, Tucson, Arizona

CONSTRUCTION

MORE ARCHITECTURAL ADVENTURES

5-1: DETECTIVE WORK: POST-AND-BEAM VS LOG CONSTRUCTION

Post-and-beam homes, log homes, and sod homes were some very early types of housing used by immigrants and pioneers. Play detective and find out whether these types of housing were used in your area and if examples still exist. Locate such houses in your community, describe where you find them, and tell who built them and when they were constructed. Remember that often post-and-beam and log houses have been covered with siding and may appear as more modern houses. Although the likelihood of finding a sod home is remote, perhaps the location and examples of them can be found through old photographs. To do your research, check various resources. Prepare a display of the results of your research for a place where you got information.

RESOURCE SHELF

- ▶ local history museum
- ▶ local historical society
- ▶ local or school library
- ▶ state historical museum
- ▶ books or old newspapers for photographs

5-2: LIFE IN A LOG HOME

Find a toy building set that uses logs. Lincoln Logs and Timberwood are two brand names you might find in a toy store. Perhaps a friend or neighbor has an old set in the garage or basement. Identify the type of notching on the toy logs. Construct a one-room house such as the early settlers might have built. If you have enough materials, enlarge the house by adding a room. Notice the changes you will have to make to attach an addition.

Now imagine it is winter, cold and snowy outside the log house. There is a large pot on a wood-burning stove at one end of the room, a wooden table and chairs in the center, and wood cots along the walls. There is no running water or electricity. The log outhouse is several yards away from the house. You are a child in a family of six living in the log home. The family needs food, water, heat, bed coverings, and a spirit of working together to survive. For one week, keep a diary that describes your life in that house. Be cautious about your wording—use language that a child of that era would use, not modern expressions. If you like, you can make the diary look more authentic by using unlined paper, dying it with coffee or a wet teabag, and letting it dry *before* you begin writing on it. You can also use a quill pen or a blunt pencil. The diaries will all be "lost" and then "recovered" by your fellow students, 200 years later. Each class member will read aloud the diary of another. Follow this reading with a discussion of the similarities and differences between the entries of various students.

5-3: My Life as a Sod House

To better understand sod homes, become one in your imagination! Think about your construction, the purposes you serve for the family that resides within your walls, and their problems. Let your imagination take you on a creative journey as you write one week's worth of entries in a diary or a poem about your life as a sod house during the rainy season. Who built you and who lives within you? To present your tale, turn off or dim the lights in the classroom, play an environmental tape or CD of a rainstorm, and read your diary or poem to the other sod houses in the class! Follow these presentations with a discussion of life under these circumstances and compare it to the life you live.

5-4: Barn-Raising: A Community Building

Life in a new country is harsh. While some families became homesteaders on land far from any neighbors, others settled in small communities. People often asked neighbors to help them in a barn-raising—everyone works together to build a structure.

The 1985 film *Witness* depicts a barn-raising in a modern Amish town. As a class, watch the portion of the video twice that shows a barn-raising. The first time, just watch. The second time, take notes, looking carefully for answers to these questions:

- What materials and tools did the Amish use? What materials and tools did you expect to see that were missing?
- How were the walls of the building constructed?
- What construction or architecture style did the Amish use?
- How was the structure assembled?
- What role did the men play? The women? The children?
- How did each role contribute to the barn-raising?

- What effect did age and gender have on participation in the construction?
- If you were a child living in that community, what would you be thinking and feeling that day?
- If it were your barn being built, what would you be thinking and feeling?

5-5: THE MAIL-ORDER HOUSE: EXAMPLES OF MASS PRODUCTION

Imagine ordering a home from a catalog! Sears and Roebuck catalog homes are found all over America. There were other catalogs that sold houses as well, such as Montgomery Ward. Try to locate them in your community.

Step 1. Find reproductions of Sears or Montgomery Ward catalogs from the 1890s through the 1920s. Look through them to find types of housing available. Note the costs of the home, including shipping and assembly.

Step 2. Think about the houses that you saw as you explored your community in other units. Photocopy some examples from the catalogs that look like some of those homes.

Step 3. Take your copies to your local historic preservation or historical society and ask if such houses were built in your community.

Step 4. When you have identified a mail-order home, make an appointment to see the home, if possible. You may need to mail a letter explaining your class assignment and requesting a visit. It is a good idea to go there with an adult. Photograph or sketch the home. If the owners will allow you inside, draw up a floor plan.

Step 5. Send a thank-you letter to the homeowners. Share the information you gathered with your class. Local historical associations will also appreciate the information.

Other American companies over the years have mass-produced homes. If you attend a large home show at a convention or exposition center, you will see them on display, often in various states of construction. Look through your community for examples later than the Sears and Roebuck homes, such as Lustron.

5-6:   BUILDING A DOME

The geodesic dome is a creative design that looks very futuristic. Buckminster Fuller tried several versions before finding one that worked well. Your challenge is to use ordinary drinking straws and string to construct a dome.

Step 1. Cut the straws into thirds and experiment with various ways to connect them. Try several geometric shapes to construct your dome.

Step 2. When you find something that works, build a dome about the size and form of half a melon or ball.

Step 3. Devise a way to mount your dome on a cardboard or foamboard base.

Step 4. Cover the dome with clear plastic wrap, aluminum foil, bubble packing wrap, cellophane, or other material. If it is interesting to look at as is, leave it uncovered. With your dome, display a card that explains the type and number of shapes you used, the number of rows you needed to achieve the height, and any other necessary, interesting information.

Step 5. Compare your completed dome with those of your classmates. Review the information cards and examine the design, balance, and structure of each dome. Tally the number of ways your classmates approached the project and evaluate the various designs.

5-7: THE RANCH HOME

The ranch style of architecture contributed to our American popular culture. After World War II, GIs returning home needed housing for themselves and their new families. The ranch-style home built in the 1950s provided for such needs. Subdivisions began when row after row of these houses were built. Working with the architectural firm you created earlier in the unit, find pictures of ranch homes in library books or period magazines. Find videotapes that depict suburban life in the 1950s. Interview adults who lived in ranch homes in the 1950s. Ask them at least the following questions:

- Where did the idea for ranch houses originate?
- Why were they so popular?
- Where were the first subdivisions built?
- What are the features of ranch homes?

Use music, mementos, photographs, advertisements, housing plans, appliances, cars, and other items in a presentation to your class.

5-8: RESEARCHING A HISTORIC HOME

Every community has what is considered the oldest home in the city or an example of an architecturally significant home. Prepare a study on a specific historic home in your community and the family who built it or had it built. Select another home in your community, either a historic landmark, an older home, or one you don't know much about. Perhaps you'll choose one threatened by demolition; your research might even help save it.

Begin by scheduling an appointment with the present owner, if possible, who may be able to provide some information. Your county recorder of deeds might also help you locate the first owner by providing you with a photocopy of the original deed. You may interview someone at your local historic preservation commission or local landmarks committee. Ask to see the forms they use when they nominate a structure for placement on a state or national historic landmark registry. Find out as much of the following information in your research as you can:

- builder and year of construction
- original number of family members
- occupation of builder or owner
- architectural style of the house
- interesting features of the house—exterior, interior, landscaping
- interior furnishings of the home at the time of construction
- relation of the house at the time of construction to the city core or outlying area
- differences between this house and others built at the same time
- major historical, cultural, and technological events at the time or in the decade of the construction
- old photographs, memorabilia of family members, or mementos of the time

With photographs and mementos (magazines, posters, artifacts) along with the material you gather in your research, present an illustrated, word-processed report to your class, historical or preservation commissions, or the local newspaper.

You have just completed a service to the community! Well done!

5-9: A RECORD OF TIME: THE HOUSES IN YOUR COMMUNITY

The American home has changed and developed over the past one hundred years. Take a visual tour of your neighborhood.

Step 1. With a camera and field notes, record the type of housing you find.

Step 2. As a class, agree upon a scale for a town of individual drawings, so you can later display them together. Sketch a number of the houses in your photographs and notes in pencil, a point marker, or colored pencils.

Step 3. With your architectural firm, review each person's sketches. Decide whether to display the houses in order by age, style, or actual location in your neighborhood.

Step 4. Cut the sketches out and arrange them on a large sheet of mural paper, using some from each contributor to get as complete a picture of your community as possible. Glue the drawings to the mural paper. Label the architectural details and other significant information.

Step 5. Post the murals in the room or in a long hallway. Take the class or another class on a tour of the neighborhood as your architectural firm sees it.

5-10: OUTSIDE THE AMERICAN HOME: LANDSCAPE, GARDENS, AND NATURAL ENVIRONMENT

The history of American landscaping provides insights into ideals for beauty, design, and outdoor activities American families enjoy. Originally, gardens were not just ornamental; they were sources of herbs and food for humans and animals. What types of designs, plantings, trees, fences, garden and lawn furniture did Americans use throughout history? Where have they located their homes in relation to the natural environment? What happens when modern urban life leaves families with little or no outdoor greenery?

Many books are set in the environments that surround American homes. Following are several, and your teacher may have some other suggestions. Choose one, being sure that three classmates will read each book. When you have finished reading your selected book, meet with the others who have read the same book. Discuss your reactions to the story itself, and then turn your attention to the garden, landscape, or yard depicted in the book. How did you picture the land in your mind's eye? As a group, create a mural that portrays the outside areas depicted in the book.

144

Include plants, trees, vegetable or flower gardens, outbuildings such as barns, outhouses, and corrals, and outdoor furniture, clotheslines, animals, and other features mentioned in the book.

BOOKLIST (COMPLETE REFERENCES ARE IN BIBLIOGRAPHY):

Caddie Woodlawn by Carol Ryrie Brink
> The true story of an eleven-year-old girl and her brothers and sisters on the Wisconsin frontier in the 1860s

Home Place by Crescent Dragonwagon
> The story of a home in a wilderness site

No Place by Kay Haugaard
> True contemporary story of groups of sixth graders who convert a dirt lot into a park in a Latino gang neighborhood

Bridge to Terabithia by Katherine Patterson
> The story of a friendship between two boys in rural Virginia

The House on Maple Street by Bonnie Pryor
> The 300-year history of a backyard garden

Homeplace by Anne Shelby
> The story of a long-ago farm

Roll of Thunder, Hear My Cry by Mildred Taylor
> The story of the importance of their land to a former slave family

Little House in the Big Woods by Laura Ingalls Wilder
> The story of family life on a Wisconsin farm at the edge of the woods

Little House on the Prairie by Laura Ingalls Wilder
> The story of family life on the prairie

5-11: TODAY'S PATTERN BOOKS AND STYLE: WHAT'S THE CONNECTION?

Pattern books or house plan books have been used for centuries. Modern examples can be found in home or building supply stores, libraries, bookstores, or magazine racks. Collect a wide variety of pattern and house plan books and bring them to school. Sharing with classmates, study the types of homes that are illustrated in the magazines.

> Step 1. Identify ten to twenty different kinds of houses.
>
> Step 2. Classify them according to the styles you studied in unit 4.
>
> Step 3. Analyze the examples and categorize them by the types you have been studying in this unit. Note the number of stories, carports or garages, and other outdoor features such as decks, patios, and porches.

Step 4. Figure out the total square footage of each house. If it cost $95.00 per square foot to build the house (the average cost in the United States), how much would each cost? Compare this to the cost listed in the original pattern books of the nineteenth century.

Step 5. What types of materials were used in the construction of each house?

Step 6. How does each home relate to its environment—city, subdivision, woods, open farmland, seaside, desert, or mountains?

Step 7. Choose the house plan you like best. Write an essay that conveys your reasons for selecting that plan. Share it with the class.

5-12: THE ENERGY-EFFICIENT HOME— A MODEL FOR THE FUTURE

The house of the future will be energy efficient and environmentally friendly. With your architectural firm, research energy-efficient methods of building that have already been invented, and perhaps propose some of your own for future construction. Consider the following factors, as well as any others you think of:

- insulation
- heating and cooling
- passive solar energy
- recycled building materials
- weather-tight windows and doors
- other features to protect against various geographical limitations (isolated from markets), natural disasters (tornado, hurricane, earthquake), and harsh climates (extreme heat or cold, wind, storms)

List the advances you have discovered. Photograph or draw the advances, or make a three-dimensional model of a home that makes use of them. Present your list, sketches, and model to the class, along with your firm's proposed innovations.

5-13: CAD: Virtual Reality in Architectural Design

One of the best innovations in architecture is computer-aided design (CAD). This tool allows architects to see their designs in three-dimensional form, rotate them on the computer screen to view them from various angles, "slice" them open to see the interior, and make changes with one keystroke. CAD allows the client to visualize the project more easily, even to walk through the rooms on the screen. If possible, arrange to visit an architect's office and see a CAD program in action.

Similar computer programs are used in designing video games or other activities that take place in and around buildings. SIMCity is one readily available software package. In a virtual reality setting, the player can move through the rooms of a building as if he or she were actually there. If you have access to virtual reality or video games that take place in or around buildings, play the game next time with an eye to its design. Notice how the buildings are constructed. Pay attention to one- and two-point perspectives that make it seem three-dimensional. Observe how the interiors appear to change as you move through them.

Imagine you are designing a new virtual reality game. The setting will be in one of the locations you have studied in this unit. The buildings will be from some era in America's past. The circumstances in the game will reflect those of the people who lived at that time. The artifacts, clothing, sounds, and dilemmas will be appropriate to the time. Work with your architectural firm to describe your virtual reality game. Name the game and explain it to the class, describing what will be seen through the eyes of the player.

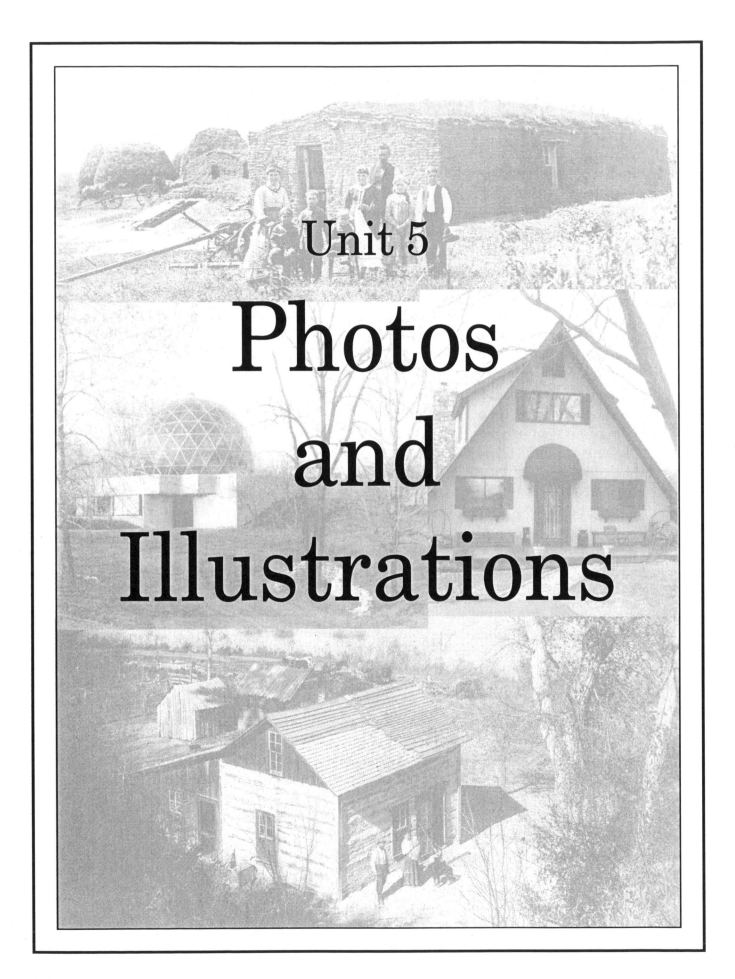

Unit 5

Photos and Illustrations

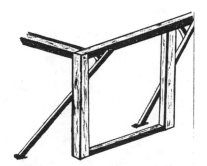

▲ **FIGURE 5-1. TIMBER FRAMES WERE USED IN THE WALL SECTIONS. Y-SHAPED POLES WERE USED TO RAISE THE TIMBERS INTO PLACE.**

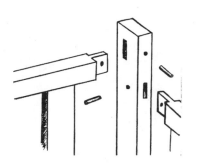

▲ **FIGURE 5-2. TIMBERS WERE SQUARED AND NOTCHED TO BE PEGGED TOGETHER.**

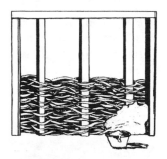

▲ **FIGURE 5-3. STICKS WERE WOVEN BETWEEN THE POLES IN THE WALL FRAME. THESE STICKS WERE CALLED WATTLE. A MIXTURE OF CLAY, WATER, AND STRAW (CALLED DAUB) FILLED IN THE SPACES BETWEEN THE WATTLE.**

▲ **FIGURE 5-4. THE ROOF WAS COVERED WITH THATCH MADE FROM BUNDLES OF STRAW AND TWIGS WOVEN AND TIED TOGETHER, AND THEN ATTACHED TO THE RAFTERS.**

▲ **FIGURE 5-5. CHIMNEYS WERE FIRST BUILT OF TIMBER, WATTLE, AND DAUB. STONE CHIMNEYS CAME LATER.**

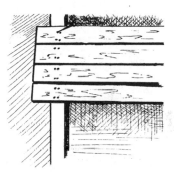

▲ **FIGURE 5-6. THE CLAPBOARDS WERE NAILED OVER THE WATTLE AND DAUB TO PROTECT THE WALLS FROM THE WEATHER.**

▲ **FIGURE 5-7. DOORS AND WINDOWS WERE CUT INTO THE FRAME. THE DOOR WAS CONSTRUCTED OF WOODEN PLANKS. THE WINDOWS WERE COVERED WITH PAPER OR CLOTH RUBBED WITH OIL.**

▲ **FIGURE 5-8. ONE HOUSE REQUIRED MANY TREES. LIMBS OF THE TREE WERE CUT OFF WITH AN AX.**

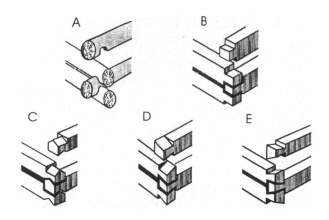

▲ FIGURE 5-9. THESE ILLUSTRATIONS ARE OF NOTCHING SYSTEMS USED IN LOG CONSTRUCTION.

▲ FIGURE 5-9A. WOOD SHINGLES, THATCH, OR BOARDS WERE ATTACHED TO THE ROOF RAFTERS. STONE OR BRICK CHIMNEYS LATER REPLACED LOG CHIMNEYS.

▲ FIGURE 5-9B. THE LOG WAS SQUARED. REMEMBER THE LENGTH AND WIDTH OF THE FRAME WERE DETERMINED BY THE SIZE OF THE LOGS.

▲ FIGURE 5-9C. THE SPACES IN BETWEEN THE LOGS WERE FILLED WITH CHINKING, A MIXTURE OF MUD, STRAW, SAND, AND LIME. WINDOWS WERE COVERED WITH OILCLOTH, AND IN LATER YEARS WITH GLASS-PANED WINDOWS.

▲ FIGURE 5-9D. THE BARK WAS REMOVED FROM THE LOGS. USING AN ADZ, THE BUILDER CHIPPED THE LOGS INTO THE DESIRED SHAPE.

▲ FIGURE 5-9E. THE FRAME WAS CREATED WITH THE LOGS. ROOF GABLES WERE ATTACHED TO THE TOP ROW OF LOGS. WINDOWS AND DOORS WERE THEN CUT IN.

▶ FIGURE 5-10. A LOG HOME-
STEAD BUILT IN 1891. IT IS
OVERLOOKING THE NIOBRARA
RIVER IN BROWN COUNTY,
NEBRASKA. NOTICE THE FAMILY
IN THE FRONT OF THEIR NICELY
CONSTRUCTED LOG HOME.
(PHOTO COURTESY OF SOLOMON
D. BUTCHER COLLECTION,
NEBRASKA STATE HISTORICAL
SOCIETY)

▶ FIGURE 5-10A. A VIEW OF
NEW SALEM, ILLINOIS, THE
PLACE ABRAHAM LINCOLN
CALLED HOME FROM 1831 TO
1934. HE LIVED IN A LOG
HOUSE SIMILAR TO THIS ONE.
HIS HOME WAS A ROOM ABOVE
A STORE, JUST LEFT OF THE BIG
BARN. (PHOTO BY E. KIDDER
SMITH)

▶ FIGURE 5-11. SOD WAS USED
AS A BUILDING MATERIAL ON THE
PLAINS OF KANSAS, NEBRASKA,
THE DAKOTAS AND EASTERN
WYOMING. THE THICK EARTHEN
WALLS PROVIDED GOOD INSULA-
TION FOR BOTH WINTER AND
SUMMER MONTHS. (PHOTO
COURTESY OF SOLOMON D.
BUTCHER COLLECTION,
NEBRASKA STATE HISTORICAL
SOCIETY)

▲ **FIGURE 5-12A.** THE FIRST STEP IN THE BRICK-MAKING PROCESS IS TO DIG THE CLAY FROM THE EARTH.

▲ **FIGURE 5-12B.** PUT THE CLAY IN A MIXING TROUGH AND ADD WATER. MIX THOROUGHLY UNTIL THICK AND PLASTIC.

▲ **FIGURE 5-12C.** POUR INTO WOODEN MOLDS AND PLACE IN THE SUN UNTIL THE MOISTURE IS BAKED OUT OF THE CLAY.

▲ **FIGURE 5-12D.** BURN WOOD IN THE KILN TO FIRE THE BRICKS FOR *24* HOURS UNTIL THEY ARE HARD. COOL, REMOVE FROM THE KILN, AND BRING TO THE BUILDING SITE.

Architecture Everywhere, © 2000 Zephyr Press, Tucson, Arizona

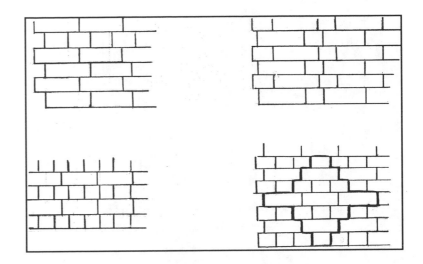

► FIGURE 5-13. BASED ON YOUR RESEARCH, IDENTIFY A. COMMON BOND, B. FLEMISH BOND, C. ENGLISH BOND, AND D. DUTCH CROSS BOND IN THE ILLUSTRATION.

► FIGURE 5-13A. LOCUST GROVE (1790) IS IN LOUISVILLE, KENTUCKY. IT WAS THE HOME OF GEORGE ROGERS CLARK FOR THE LAST NINE YEARS OF HIS LIFE. (PHOTO COURTESY OF HABS)

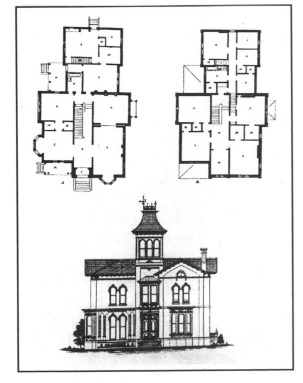

◄ FIGURE 5-14. ONE COULD HAVE MR. BICKNELL CUSTOM DESIGN A HOUSE AS SEEN HERE IN AN 1870 PLAN. WHAT ROOMS CAN YOU IDENTIFY ON THE FIRST FLOOR? HOW ABOUT THE SECOND FLOOR? YOU MAY NEED TO USE A MAGNIFYING GLASS.

◄ FIGURE 5-15. HERE IS A ONE-AND-A-HALF STORY HOME ORDERED FROM THE *1908* SEARS AND ROEBUCK CATALOG AND BUILT IN EDWARDSVILLE, ILLINOIS.

◄ FIGURE 5-16. QUONSET HUTS, CORRUGATED, HALF-ROUNDED METAL BUILDINGS, WERE QUICK AND INEXPENSIVE FORMS OF HOUSING. THEY WERE USED IN WORLD WAR II AND FOUND ADDITIONAL USES IN THE UNITED STATES AFTER THE WAR.

◄ FIGURE 5-17. MOBILE HOMES ARE ANOTHER EXAMPLE OF INEXPENSIVE AND PRACTICAL HOUSING. THEY BECAME POPULAR IN THE *1940s* WHEN THERE WAS A GREAT NEED FOR HOUSING AFTER WORLD WAR II.

▶ *FIGURE 5-18. THE A-FRAME IS A UNIQUE FORM OF HOUSING, OFTEN USED FOR VACATION HOMES.*

▶ *FIGURE 5-19. ARCHITECT BUCKMINSTER FULLER CREATED THE GEODESIC DOME. HERE HE USED IT IN THE RELIGIOUS CENTER ON THE CAMPUS OF SOUTHERN ILLINOIS UNIVERSITY AT EDWARDSVILLE, ILLINOIS.*

▶ *FIGURE 5-20. THE ONE-STORY RANCH-STYLE HOME WITH CARPORT WAS THE ANSWER TO THE NEED FOR AFFORDABLE HOUSING AFTER WORLD WAR II.*

◀ FIGURE 5-21. A SPLIT-LEVEL HOME ALLOWS FOR THE BASEMENT OR LOWER LEVEL TO BE USED FOR LIVING SPACE. SINCE THE ENTRANCE IS SPLIT BETWEEN THE TWO LEVELS, THE HOUSE HAS LITTLE WASTED ROOM.

▶ FIGURE 5-22A. THIS APARTMENT BUILDING IS SEVEN STORIES TALL AND OVERLOOKS A LARGE PARK. ITS FRONT IS DESIGNED WITH MANY ROUNDED BAYS TO BRING IN LOTS OF LIGHT. IT WAS BUILT IN 1907, AND EACH UNIT HAS NINE ROOMS.

◀ FIGURE 5-22B. THIS COMPLEX IS A HIGH-RISE APARTMENT BUILDING. HOW MANY FLOORS DOES IT HAVE? IT IS CONSTRUCTED OF STEEL, GLASS, CEMENT, AND STONE. HOW MANY ELEVATORS WOULD YOU NEED TO SERVICE THIS BUILDING?

Architecture Everywhere, © 2000 Zephyr Press, Tucson, Arizona

▲ *FIGURE 5-22C. THERE ARE MANY TYPES OF PUBLIC HOUSING PROJECTS TO SERVE THE NEEDS OF PEOPLE TODAY. THIS EXAMPLE IS DESIGNED TO MAKE A STATEMENT ABOUT THE USE OF MATERIALS, TEXTURES, AND SHAPES TO CREATE AN ATTRACTIVE PLACE TO LIVE.*

▲ *FIGURE 5-22D. MANY PROFESSIONAL PEOPLE AND OLDER AMERICANS LIKE TO LIVE IN SMALLER PATIO HOMES THAT REQUIRE MINIMAL MAINTENANCE BUT STILL CREATE AN ATTRACTIVE ENVIRONMENT. SOMETIMES THESE HOMES ARE ATTACHED TO ONE ANOTHER. THIS TYPE OF HOUSING ALLOWS INDIVIDUALS TO SPEND TIME IN OTHER PLACES AND TAKE PART IN A VARIETY OF ACTIVITIES.*

▲ FIGURE 5-23A. THE HOUSE OF THE TWENTY-
FIRST CENTURY WILL STILL LOOK LIKE A HOUSE
AND BE DESIGNED TO MEET THE NEEDS OF THE
INFORMAL LIFESTYLES OF THE AMERICAN FAMILY.
(ILLUSTRATION COURTESY OF BLOODGOOD SHARP
BUSTER, ARCHITECTS AND PLANNERS, INC.)

▲ FIGURE 5-23B. THE REAR OF THE HOME OF THE
TWENTY-FIRST CENTURY FEATURES RECYCLING AREAS,
POCKET-SIZED VEGETABLE GARDENS, PATIOS FOR
PLAYING AND LIVING, AND EVEN A LAP POOL.
(ILLUSTRATION COURTESY OF BLOODGOOD SHARP
BUSTER, ARCHITECTS AND PLANNERS, INC.)

◀ FIGURE 5-23C. DINING ROOM, LIVING
ROOM, KITCHEN, AND DEN WILL BECOME
ONE VAST ROOM FOR MULTIFUNCTIONAL
FAMILY LIVING AND COMMUNICATION.
(ILLUSTRATION COURTESY OF BLOODGOOD
SHARP BUSTER, ARCHITECTS AND
PLANNERS, INC.).

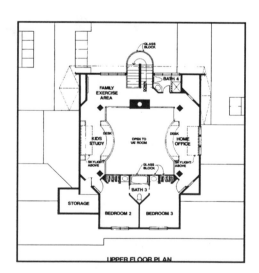

▲ FIGURE 5-23D. NOTICE THE EMPHASIS ON
INFORMAL LIVING ACTIVITIES IN THIS MAIN FLOOR
PLAN OF THE TWENTY-FIRST CENTURY HOUSE.
(ILLUSTRATION COURTESY OF BLOODGOOD SHARP
BUSTER, ARCHITECTS AND PLANNERS, INC.)

▲ FIGURE 5-23E. IN THIS UPPER-LEVEL FLOOR PLAN
OF THE TWENTY-FIRST CENTURY HOUSE, FAMILY
ACTIVITY AREAS ARE ON ONE END AND SLEEPING
AREAS ON THE OTHER. EXERCISE AND STUDY AREAS
HAVE BEEN SPECIFICALLY DESIGNED FOR THE FAMILY.
(ILLUSTRATION COURTESY OF BLOODGOOD SHARP
BUSTER, ARCHITECTS AND PLANNERS, INC.)

Unit 6

Want to Become an Architect?

Creating with Form and Function

By definition, a building is a sculpture, because it is a three-dimensional object.

—Frank O. Gehry

FOUNDATION

IN THIS UNIT, STUDENTS

- EXAMINE THE ROLE OF THE ARCHITECT IN DESIGNING AND BUILDING.

- CONSIDER THE ISSUES THAT FACE THE ARCHITECT AND THE PROCESS THAT HE OR SHE GOES THROUGH TO SERVE THE NEEDS OF THE PEOPLE WHO WILL USE THE BUILDING.

- STUDY TWO FAMOUS AMERICAN ARCHITECTS, FRANK O. GEHRY AND ROBERT A.M. STERN, AND THEIR DIVERSE APPROACHES TO DESIGN.

- EXPLORE THE ELEMENTS AND PRINCIPLES OF AESTHETICS A DESIGNER AND ARCHITECT USE TO CREATE A PLEASING AND FUNCTIONAL BUILDING.

- CREATE THEIR OWN BUILDINGS OR ARCHITECTURAL STRUCTURES USING A VARIETY OF MATERIALS.

FRANK LLOYD WRIGHT'S 1937 MASTERPIECE, FALLINGWATER

VISITING WITH THE ARCHITECT: FORM, FUNCTION, AND THE CLIENT

DESIGN

MAIN IDEAS IN THIS CHAPTER

- The architect is a trained professional who designs buildings for clients.
- Because they are artists, architects have a unique style or approach that makes their designs different from those of other architects.
- Architects use the elements and principles of art and design to make their structures visually pleasing and interesting, to make them fit into the environment.

MATERIALS

► figures 6-1 through 6-4 (see page 189 for enlarged figures)

FIGURE 6-1

FIGURE 6-2

FIGURE 6-3

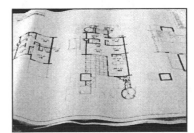

FIGURE 6-4

RESOURCE SHELF

► books on contemporary American architects
► videos and exhibits on contemporary architecture and building
► local chapter of the American Institute of Architecture (for a visit to an architect's office and/or presentation to the class)

BLUEPRINTS
Visiting with the Architect:
Form, Function, and the Client

Photocopy the following section for students to read or read it aloud to them.

After completing the units, you understand your sense of place and appreciate the history and types of architecture that make up our humanmade world. Now you can become architects to create your own structures.

An architect is a person who has been trained to design and supervise the construction of buildings. The architect works in an office to design and create plans, models, reports, and illustrations, and to hold conferences with clients and other staff. Study figure 6-1 and list all the objects and working tools you see in the architect's office.

To design functional, safe, and aesthetically pleasing buildings, architects are trained in many areas: design, physics, mathematics, sociology, architectural history, and engineering. The buildings they design must conform to state and local building codes. The buildings must also satisfy health standards, take into account local weather and climate conditions, and accommodate those with disabilities. Architects are also trained to plan the environment that surrounds building. Since they design buildings for many uses, they are concerned about the impact of that use on the surrounding spaces, the ways the building will fit with other buildings on the block or lot, and whether the space is too small or large for a structure.

These are the steps an architect takes to complete a building:

Step 1. Ascertain the client's need for a building and gather information, such as the available budget.

Step 2. Create drawings and models to help the client visualize the building design. For example, figure 6-2 shows the design for the interior of a gymnasium, and figure 6-3 is a model of another building built to scale. The client reviews the designs, sketches, or plans from time to time and tells the architect what he or she likes and doesn't like about the proposed building.

Step 3. Make changes to the plan according to the client's responses.

Step 4. Finalize the design for approval by the client.

Step 5. Translate the designs into *blueprints* such as those in figure 6-4, which are the floor plans of a building and the drawings of the outside of the structure from all sides. This step may also be completed by a draftsperson.

Step 6. Prepare plans for a basement, crawl space, or foundation, and for electricity, plumbing, heating, and air conditioning.

Step 7. Submit the project to building contractors for cost estimates. Usually the lowest bid receives the contract.

Step 8. Supervise the construction to ensure that the contractor follows the blueprints and other designs.

With a partner, decide who will be the client and who will be the architect. The client tells the architect what he or she likes or doesn't like about the interior design and the model in figures 6-2 and 6-3. For the purposes of this exercise, you can assume that the model in figure 6-3 shows the exterior of the gymnasium complex. What would you ask your partner, the architect, to change? The architect responds to the client's input. How would you incorporate the ideas into your plan?

CONSTRUCTION
MORE ARCHITECTURAL ADVENTURES

Two Great American Architects

Design

Main Ideas in This Chapter

- Frank O. Gehry and Robert A.M. Stern are two prominent contemporary architects whose styles are very different.
- Each of these architects is influenced by the environment and the beliefs he holds about the purpose of architecture.
- Architects use elements and principles of design to convey certain qualities in their buildings.

Materials

▶ figures 6-5 through 6-6 (see page 190 for enlarged photos)

FIGURE 6-5

FIGURE 6-6

▶ books, pictures, videos, or magazine articles on Frank O. Gehry and Robert A.M. Stern

Guidelines for Instruction

Decide whether you want students to research contemporary American architects in addition to the ones they will research here. They can choose one from the sidebar list.

BLUEPRINTS
Two Great American Architects

Photocopy the following section for students to read or read it aloud to them.

Architects, like other artists, get their ideas for buildings by exploring and experimenting. While initially "playing around" with materials (see sidebar, page 165), ideas about buildings and their forms begin to take shape.

CONTEMPORARY AMERICAN ARCHITECTS

- *I. M. PEI*
- *MAYA LIN*
- *RICHARD MEIER*
- *PETER EISENMAN*
- *HELMUT JAHN*
- *ROBERT VENTURI*
- *CHARLES MOORE*
- *ANTOINE PREDOCK*
- *ARQUITECTONICA*
- *STANLEY TIGERMAN*
- *HUGH JACOBSEN*

As architects look at and move around two-dimensional sketches or three-dimensional objects, the arrangement often spurs them to think of the models as types of buildings—an interesting house, a shelter for a park, a museum, an office building. The architect uses imagination to visualize how these concepts or arrangements of shapes and forms can be used as a building or structure.

Although architects create many buildings, each new building starts off in the planning stage, as if it were the first building architects ever designed. They begin by processing many ideas, experimenting with art materials, seeking to establish or express a certain look or style that is their trademark. The work of the contemporary architects we study here is well respected. You will research their approaches and compare and contrast their styles.

MATERIALS

- *PAPER*
- *PAINT*
- *INK*
- *MARKERS*
- *CLAY*
- *FOAM*
- *OLD CARDBOARD BOXES*
- *PHOTOGRAPHS OF BUILDINGS*
- *FAVORITE NATURAL OBJECTS*
- *COLLECTABLE ITEMS FROM OUR TIME, SUCH AS A SODA CAN*

FRANK O. GEHRY

I fantasize in sketches. After the drawings are made, lots of models follow. Initially the models are made from paper shapes bent, folded, curved and shaped to the desired form.

Gehry lives and works in Santa Monica, California, and has developed an approach to architecture that is associated with *deconstructivism.* Look up that term in the glossary or find it in an architecture book. After you understand the elements of deconstructivism, you will be able to understand Gehry's approach to designing buildings. Figure 6-5 is a model of Gehry's design for the proposed Walt Disney Concert Hall to be built in Los Angeles.

- What do you think of this model as a piece of architecture?
- Where do you suppose Gehry gets his ideas for his buildings?
- What effects do you think living around Los Angeles has had on Gehry's thinking?
- What makes his use of form and space unique?
- What materials do you think he will use to build the concert hall?
- What type of balance does Gehry use? (Check the glossary, page 206, for assistance.)
- What various textures do you see?
- How tall will the concert hall be?

Gehry has created many buildings all over the world. A recent building in Spain was acclaimed as a masterpiece. Find a picture of the building and share it with your classmates.

ROBERT A.M. STERN

I see the styles and monuments of earlier times as the vocabulary and grammar of the language of architecture but the syntax and diction are of this time and my own.

Stern lives and works in New York City. His approach to architecture is postmodern, which was discussed in unit 5. Look at figure 6-6. This building is a library for St. Paul's School in Concord, New Hampshire, which students your age use. Compare this building to Gehry's concert hall.

- How does Stern use shape and form?
- What type of balance does he use? (Check the glossary, page 206, for assistance.)
- How does Stern use texture and pattern?
- How and where are traditional aspects of architecture incorporated into the building's design?
- What types of other buildings from other times influenced Stern in his design of this building?
- How does it fit into the environment?
- How does the design of the building reflect the landscape of the East Coast and the humanmade environment there?
- Does the building reveal that Stern has a strong sense of place? How can you tell?
- How are Stern's building and Gehry's building similar and different?

Compare and contrast other buildings designed by these two architects. Identify the working method or approach each used to design the buildings. Look at the shapes and forms each one uses. Describe the feelings that you get from their work. Evaluate their buildings as to how well they serve the purpose for which they were designed. Although their work is quite different, their designs are very successful. Why is that true?

CONSTRUCTION
MORE ARCHITECTURAL ADVENTURES

6-7: Deconstruction: A Modern Approach (page 177)

DESIGN ELEMENTS AND PRINCIPLES

DESIGN

MAIN IDEAS IN THIS SECTION

- Architects use the same elements and principles of design as other visual artists.
- Architectural design incorporates the elements of line, shape, form, texture, pattern, and color to create a visually pleasing or interesting building.
- The principles of balance, proportion, emphasis, and rhythm help the architect convey an overall message.

MATERIALS:

▶ figures 6-7 through 6-21 (see pages 191–194 for enlarged photos)

▶ photocopies of drawing techniques from appendix (page 203)

BLUEPRINTS

DESIGN ELEMENTS AND PRINCIPLES

Photocopy the following section for students to read or read it aloud to them.

For architects to design effective, artistically interesting, beautiful buildings, they must be able to apply the elements and principles of art or design to architecture. The architects you have studied are masters in the application of these elements and principles. Now you will briefly review these elements and principles and see examples of them. Each is followed by one or more activities to help you apply the elements and exercise your creativity by using various media and processes.

USING LINE IN BUILDING DESIGN

Lines are continuous marks made by a pencil, pen, or paintbrush. In addition to applied lines made by art tools, lines can be undrawn, such as those that form the outline of the objects around us. Lines are everywhere in our environment. They are found in nature as well as in our humanmade world. For example, a leaf has lines that create its outline. Figure 6-7 illustrates the additional lines a leaf and branches have: twigs, shadows of the twigs, and the veins of the leaf. In a building, the lines help us to contain the building or parts of buildings in our minds. Certain elements in the building illustrate types of lines, such as you see in figure 6-8. Notice the sweeping, curved line of the staircase railing and the zig-zag line created by the stair treads that curve upward.

FIGURE 6-7

FIGURE 6-8

Look around the classroom and identify dominant lines that define the room. Do the same with trees and bushes on the campus, and with buildings in the neighborhood.

CONSTRUCTION
MORE ARCHITECTURAL ADVENTURES

6-8: Working with Lines to Express Feelings (page 177)

6-9: Identifying Dominant Lines in Architecture (page 177)

USING SHAPE IN BUILDING DESIGN

Shapes are usually *two-dimensional*, that is, they have only length and width. Architects and builders use geometric and organic shapes. Geometric shapes are those used in geometry (see sidebar). Notice in figure 6-9 how the circle and rectangle are used to create a skylight.

FIGURE 6-9

SOME GEOMETRIC SHAPES

CIRCLES
OVALS
SQUARES
TRIANGLES
RECTANGLES
HEXAGONS
OCTAGONS
HALF CIRCLES

SOME ORGANIC SHAPES

LEAVES
SEASHELLS
SNOWFLAKES
HONEYCOMBS
PLANT STRUCTURES
DANDELIONS
BUBBLE CELLS
ANIMALS

Organic shapes are those found in nature and are often used to add decorative interest to buildings (see sidebar). What organic shapes, both animal and plant, do you see interwoven in the metal bas relief panel in figure 6-10? How do they affect you?

FIGURE 6-10

CONSTRUCTION:
MORE ARCHITECTURAL ADVENTURES

6-10: Variations on a Shape: What a Neat Design! (page 178)

6-11: A Study in Cubism: What You Can Do with a Box (page 178)

6-12: Creating a Hotel for Mother Nature; or Variations on the Seashell Hotel (page 178)

6-13: Using Organic and Geometric Shapes in Architectural Design (page 178)

USING FORM IN BUILDING DESIGN

Two-dimensional shapes have length and width. When depth is added, the shapes become *three-dimensional* forms. Buildings are forms. They usually have a top, a bottom, a side, a front, and a back. Stacking a series of two-dimensional squares to the same height as the squares are wide creates a cube, which has depth. Stacking a series of two-dimensional circles of the same size creates a cylinder. A cone is a stack of graduated sizes of circles.

Note that the form of the park pavilion's top in figure 6-11 looks like an onion plant. What forms do you notice in figure 6-12? How do you think they were made? What purposes do they serve?

FIGURE 6-11

FIGURE 6-12

How many geometric and organic forms can you find in the humanmade environment around your city? List them and compare your list with those of your classmates.

CONSTRUCTION

MORE ARCHITECTURAL ADVENTURES

6-14: A Towering Form (page 179)

USING TEXTURE IN BUILDING DESIGN

FIGURE 6-13

Texture is the tactile surface of an object, the feel one gets when touching the surface of the object. In nature, as in architecture, there are many textural surfaces that create many tactile sensations (see sidebars). Figure 6-13 shows the smooth, reflecting surface of glass in an office building. Notice how the texture of the glass gives the reflected buildings a wavy appearance.

SMOOTH SURFACES
GLASS
STAINLESS STEEL
PLASTERED WALLS
POLISHED MARBLE
CERAMIC TILE
SANDED WOOD

ROUGH SURFACES
BRICK
STONE
WOOD AND ASPHALT SHINGLES
ROUGH SAWED WOOD
CONCRETE BLOCKS

FIGURE 6-14

Contrast the texture of glass with the texture of field stone used on the wall of a shopping center. Figure 6-14 is a close-up photograph of the wall's surface. We notice textures with our eyes as well as our fingers. Our eyes give us clues about surface qualities, and often surfaces give us a fine sense of pleasure or beauty. The presence of sunlight or artificial light determines the degree to which we can see texture.

CONSTRUCTION
MORE ARCHITECTURAL ADVENTURES

USING PATTERN IN BUILDING DESIGN

> ### EXAMPLES OF RADIAL PATTERN
> *A NAUTILUS SEASHELL*
> *A HONEYCOMB*
> *THE SUN*
> *A SAND DOLLAR*
> *AN ORANGE*

When lines, colors, shapes, and forms are carefully planned, arranged, and repeated, the result is a pattern. Patterns can be *regular,* with geometric lines, shapes, forms, and textures organized in a series of designs that are repeated over and over again in a ceiling, wall surface, frieze (a decorated band along the upper part of a wall), or roof. *Irregular* patterns can also be created from the same elements in an asymmetrical balance.

Pattern, like shape and form, is found in nature. Architects often imitate natural patterns in buildings. Figure 6-15 shows an example of a radial pattern—the design radiates from the center and moves out. Why do you think the architect put this strong pattern in this tall, open space? In

FIGURE 6-15   **FIGURE 6-16**

figure 6-16 you can see the influence of a nautilus shell on architecture. This photograph depicts the inside of the space seen in figure 6-12.

CONSTRUCTION
MORE ARCHITECTURAL ADVENTURES

USING COLOR IN BUILDING DESIGN

Color influences a mood. Architects use color to create an appropriate mood for the building: a shopping mall will have different colors than a church. When we see and use a building, the colors used in the building have an impact on our emotions.

Architects emphasize color in their structures to evoke a certain mood or feeling. They use bright, primary colors to create feelings of happiness, celebration, joy, fun, and youth.

> ### PRIMARY COLORS
> *BLUE*
> *RED*
> *YELLOW*

If you get the TV station Nickelodeon in your home, have you noticed the colors that are used on its shows? Acid greens and blues are everywhere, creating an upbeat, fun-filled mood. Often the walls, fabric coverings, cabinetry, and surface tops in hospitals, clinics, and doctors' offices are muted to create a calming or peaceful mood.

MUTED OR SUBDUED COLORS

PLUM
DEEP BURGUNDY
GRAY
BLUE-GRAY
CORAL
PEACH

MATERIALS EVOKING ELEGANCE, CLASS, GRANDEUR

STONE
FIRED BRICK
OILED WOOD
POLISHED WOOD

Natural materials emit rich colors and tones. Humanmade products such as steel, chrome, plastic, and laminate are used extensively in architecture. Each material has its own particular color and texture, and creates a special effect. Wood shingles painted white represent a truly American feel, mood, and look.

To see how color affects mood, try this experiment.

Step 1. Take an inventory of the way color is used inside and outside of buildings around you. Include such places as your classroom, bedroom, dentist's office, library, video arcade, toy or party store, elegant restaurant, and fast-food stand.

Step 2. Fold a sheet of white paper lengthwise into four columns. In the leftmost column, list ten rooms or buildings that you observed.

Step 3. Get a box of crayons with at least 64 colors. In the second column, color in a box for each room you listed with the primary color used in that room. Notice the mood that the colors create. How does that mood suit the room or building?

Step 4. Now empty the crayons into a paper bag or other container and randomly select a crayon from the bag. In the third column, make a colored box for the first item on the list. Look at the color and imagine being in that particular room if it were painted that color instead of the color in column 2. How would you feel in the room if it were that color? Would that mood be right for that type of room or building? Select another crayon at random and color with it in the last column. Again, notice the atmosphere that would be created for that room and question whether it would feel right.

Step 5. Repeat with other crayons drawn from the bag for each of the rooms listed.

Step 6. Compare your rooms, colors, and the moods you experienced with others in your class. What did you learn from this experiment?

CONSTRUCTION
MORE ARCHITECTURAL ADVENTURES

USING BALANCE TO CREATE INTERESTING STRUCTURES

Essentially there are two types of balance: symmetrical and asymmetrical. In architecture, *symmetrical balance* refers to buildings that have equal elements and features on both sides of a central point. An equal number of doors, windows, roof gables, shutters, and so on is found in each section. The mass or weight of each section would be the same as well. The building in figure 6-17 is an example of symmetrical balance.

FIGURE 6-17

FIGURE 6-18

Asymmetrical balance refers to architecture that has an unequal balance. There is an uneven number of elements on each side of the imaginary line. The high-rise building in figure 6-18 shows asymmetrical balance. One half of the building is very different from the other half in terms of both space and form. It is as though the architect carved into the inner core to create this unusual use of asymmetrical balance.

> As you walk down the street, notice which buildings demonstrate symmetrical balance and which demonstrate asymmetrical balance. What elements help you decide? How does the balance used suit each building's purpose?

CONSTRUCTION
MORE ARCHITECTURAL ADVENTURES

USING PROPORTION TO CREATE INTERESTING STRUCTURES

Perhaps the most complicated element in architecture is *proportion*. Proportion is a sense of order created out of the elements and principles of art. It is the selection and arrangement of shape to shape, form to form, texture to texture, and the relationship of these to each other. Sometimes the standard sizes of materials used in building dictate what shapes and forms must be used; therefore, some decisions are already made. Examples are doors, windows, and roof trusses. However, the architect still must decide where the doors or windows will be placed in the front, back, and sides of the building, and what relationship they will have to the rest of the building.

To determine this relationship, the architect often prepares sketches, drawings, or even models. After seeing the relationship of all the elements to each other in a plan or model, the architect determines the final proportions and relationship.

> The Greeks used a formula called *the golden rectangle* to design buildings according to an ideal sense of proportion. Find out what this formula is, and find it in famous American buildings.

The architect, like the artist, uses the eye as frequently as using geometry to create proportion. When you see a building or set of buildings, no doubt its beauty and feeling of completeness reflect its sense of proportion. Can you think of a building that has pleasing proportions? Many people feel that Frank Lloyd Wright's house *Fallingwater,* seen in figure 6-19, is a very good example of architecture that exhibits fine proportions.

FIGURE 6-19

CONSTRUCTION
MORE ARCHITECTURAL ADVENTURES

6-24: Making the Best Fantasy Castle (page 183)

6-25: A Makeover for Your City (page 183)

USING EMPHASIS TO CREATE INTERESTING STRUCTURES

Just as writers do, architects emphasize various elements of their work. Writers do it with punctuation marks: an exclamation mark signifies excitement; a question mark follows a sentence that asks a question.

FIGURE 6-20

Architects may use one color or shape to stand out among an arrangement of other shapes or colors. A dominant shape might differ quite markedly from other shapes. In figure 6-20, the architect used three circles to emphasize the wall of an office complex. The landscape architect also placed the tree to emphasize the wall and space.

<u>CONSTRUCTION</u>
MORE ARCHITECTURAL ADVENTURES

USING RHYTHM TO CREATE INTERESTING STRUCTURES

FIGURE 6-21

When architects repeat a shape or form, using a specific line or texture repeatedly, they give the building a type of rhythm. Rhythm has to do with the elements used to simulate movement.

Figure 6-21 illustrates a rhythm through the repetitive rounded arch forms and sculptured decorative motifs around the base of the building. A sense of vertical movement is created by columns around a building, such as those in the Greek or Roman style found in many government buildings. Contemporary artists, too, use rhythm in their work. Look for examples of rhythm in the buildings around your town. Remember the key word—*repetition*.

EXAMPLES OF RHYTHM

REPETITION OF A ROUNDED ARCH
REPETITION OF COLUMNS OF THE SAME SIZE
VARIATION OF LINES OR SHAPES WITH THE PATTERN REPEATED

<u>CONSTRUCTION</u>
MORE ARCHITECTURAL ADVENTURES

Architecture Everywhere, © 2000 Zephyr Press, Tucson, Arizona

CONSTRUCTION

MORE ARCHITECTURAL ADVENTURES

6-1: DESIGNING A BUSINESS PLAN

You are a client who wants an architect to design a new fitness center for you and your company. Before you interview architects, you must have a business plan. Meet with a small group of classmates other than those who were in your architecture firm. The group will serve as the board of directors for your company and answer the following questions.

- What kind of company are you? What do you need in your fitness center? Write down your needs and the specific features you want.
- How much money do you have to spend? Do you have the fund or will your company need to borrow money?
- Where is the proposed building site? Does your company own the lot, or will you need to borrow the money to buy the lot as well?
- Who will use the fitness center? Will they pay dues to support the center, or will your company or an agency (such as a school district, hospital, or church) pay the expenses of running the center?
- To operate your center, you'll need enough money to cover annual expenses—mortgage payments, electricity, water, staff. Calculate those expenses. If your building must produce income, what dues will you charge your members? How many members would you need? Would you be able to generate enough money on a yearly basis to pay back your loan and the expenses of running the center? If so, you are ready to visit with a number of architects.

6-2: INTERVIEWING AN ARCHITECT

You will need some important pieces of information to decide which architectural firm to hire. Meet with your board of directors to list questions you will ask the architect to determine if the firm is right for you. For example, you might want to know about the architect's background, building processes, fees the firm will charge you, construction schedules, and so on. Compare your list to those created by other groups in your class.

6-3: DESIGNING A NEW THEME PARK

This is your opportunity to be very creative. With your architectural firm, design a theme park just for middle school students. Start by brainstorming the things you like to do best at your favorite parks. Record these ideas and look for a theme that can tie them all together (for example, rock music, skateboards, horseback riding). Come up with names for the rides or other activities that might be in this park, and a name for the theme park itself. On what kind of land would your park work best—flat, rolling, hilly, or a combination? With your architectural firm, sketch the park on large mural paper using a scale of 1 inch = 1 foot. Post your mural in the class for other groups to see.

6-4: CREATING THE TEAPOT HOUSE
OR OTHER UNUSUAL HABITATS

Since your early childhood, you have read stories in which certain little animals, make-believe creatures, and nursery rhyme characters live in unusual houses. The lady who lived in a shoe is a good example. Now is your chance to design some unusual structures for some unusual clients. Using clay, wood, polystyrene, cardboard, sugar cubes, soda cans, corks, or other objects, create a building with one of the following themes.

- Create a structure that represents what you would look like if you were a building.
- Create a factory that resembles the product being produced.
- Create a mailbox house for a postman.
- Create a high-rise birdhouse for our spring and summer feathered friends.
- Create the ultimate teapot house.
- Create a house for a pixie.

6-5: MY FAVORITE STORY IN BUILDING FORM

We all have a favorite story. What would that story look like if it took the form of a building? Think of the characters in the story. What part of the building would they become? What would cover or decorate the outside of the building? How would it take on the mood or place of the story? Use the materials that best fit the story and its characters. Draw or construct a scale model of this fanciful building. Hold a story circle with the rest of your class. All of you share your story-buildings in turn. Perhaps your classmates will recognize your story from the appearance of the building.

Architecture Everywhere, © 2000 Zephyr Press, Tucson, Arizona

6-6: A Song (or Other Medium) Becomes a Building

Think of your favorite songs (movies, poems, or stories). Select one that includes a description of a building, special place, or home. Imagine how the building looks. See it in your mind's eye. Create this make-believe structure in a painting or model. Include the people, animals, or other elements.

Now think of an interesting building, perhaps one you have seen while learning about architecture. Compose a song or write a poem that conveys your feelings about the building—the mood it creates, the people who occupy it, some activities that take place there. Sing your song or read your poem to the class.

6-7: Deconstruction: A Modern Approach

Now that you have some familiarity with deconstructivism, use it to create either a drawing or model. Use whatever materials you feel would best convey the philosophy of this approach. Display your project beside one of your earlier drawings or models. Write a brief comparison of the two.

6-8: Working with Lines to Express Feelings

Lines are all around us. Architects use lines to create many different effects and feelings. Gather a variety of drawing materials: soft pencil, marker, fine-tipped pen, tempera paint, and half-inch brushes. On a large sheet of paper, make as many types of lines as you can: thick, thin, straight, curvy, wavy, curly, dotted, angular, broken, and pointed. After you have experimented, take a new sheet of paper and create a line composition. Repeat two or three kinds of lines to create a particular feeling.

6-9: Identifying Dominant Lines in Architecture

This exercise will help with your perception and analysis of lines in buildings. Find ten photographs of buildings in magazines. Trim them into clean rectangles or squares. Use a glue stick to arrange the photographs on a piece of white paper. Analyze each building to pick out the dominant lines—the strongest lines, which define the shape or form of the building. In many buildings these will be straight lines, but you may have found some pictures where the dominant lines are curved. Now take a wide black marker and draw a line on top of the dominant lines in each photograph. A ruler might help with the straight lines.

6-10: VARIATIONS ON A SHAPE: WHAT A NEAT DESIGN!

Choose one geometric shape other than a square or rectangle (circle, triangle, oval, diamond, polygon). Select one type of building other than a house, such as a library, store, or hospital. Create a floor plan for this building using only the one shape you have selected. Use graph paper and colored pencils or thin-tipped markers. Be as creative as you can with your shape. Display your drawings in class, first with others that used the same shape, and then with those who designed a similar type of building. Evaluate how well the designers used the shapes in their buildings. Select the ones you think work best together. Defend the reasons for your opinions.

6-11: A STUDY IN CUBISM: WHAT YOU CAN DO WITH A BOX

The Dutch artist Piet Mondrian (1872–1944) arranged squares and rectangles into asymmetrical designs in his paintings. He separated the primary-colored shapes with thick black horizontal and vertical lines. Mondrian influenced a lot of architects. Study Mondrian's work. Then use primary-colored and white construction paper to translate his approach into a three-dimensional model of a building. Remember to outline or accent with black strips. Display your cubist architecture in the classroom.

6-12: CREATING A HOTEL FOR MOTHER NATURE; OR VARIATIONS ON THE SEASHELL HOTEL

Select a natural shape such as a shell and consider how you could use the shape to design a hotel building. What would the floor plan of the hotel look like? What special features in the hotel would complement the seashell form? Draw your plan on paper. Identify the rooms of the hotel. Post your drawing on Hotel Row in your classroom.

6-13: USING ORGANIC AND GEOMETRIC SHAPES IN ARCHITECTURAL DESIGN

Study the architecture of Frank Lloyd Wright and Bruce Goff. Both use combinations of organic and geometric shapes. Select various pre-cut geometric and organic pasteboard shapes and experiment, arranging them to create an architectural model. Place the model on a baseboard and draw in or use landscaping material from a local hobby shop to construct the exterior landscape, including trees, shrubs, and other plants.

    Architecture Everywhere, © 2000 Zephyr Press, Tucson, Arizona

6-14: A TOWERING FORM

Create a three-dimensional abstract building from objects you find.

Step 1. Gather several small, discarded geometrical objects such as rubber balls, soda cans, milk cartons, yogurt containers, toy blocks, and tiny gift boxes. Look around your house, garage, or yard to find them.

Step 2. Stack your objects to create a tower. You may need to try several different arrangements to get one that will stay upright and look pleasing. Use hot glue or double-sided masking tape to hold the objects together.

Step 3. Look at your tower from all sides and select the most interesting angle. Sketch your three-dimensional form on paper, using two-point perspective.

6-15: CREATING SURFACE TEXTURES FOR BUILDINGS

This activity will help you see and use textures in designing buildings.

Step 1. Cut out from old magazines a wide variety of textures of all types and colors. Do not be concerned with what the objects are; simply look for the textures.

Step 2. On a 12-by-18-inch poster board, lightly draw a building— a house, hotel, office building, or church.

Step 3. Cut out and arrange the textures onto the building you have drawn. Use a variety of textures, colors, and shapes to create an interesting effect. When you are satisfied with the appearance, paste the textures onto the sketch.

Step 4. Display your picture with others in the class and see the ways texture on a building impacts you.

6-16: FINDING TEXTURES IN BUILDINGS

Find out what textures look like when found in the world around us.

Step 1. Take some old crayons—the thick kind that small children use are ideal—and peel the paper from them.

Step 2. Find flat objects in nature, such as leaves. Put the leaf on a flat surface and place a piece of white paper over it. Use the side of the crayon to rub over the surface of the paper with the object underneath. The object's outline and other textures will appear. Do the same with humanmade objects such as bricks, wire mesh, and coins.

Step 3. Cut the rubbed images out and arrange them in a collage on another sheet of paper. Use the rubbings to create a building. Mount the compositions and arrange them in the room. Check out the variety.

6-17: CREATING WHIMSICAL ARCHITECTURE IN CLAY

Using clay slab construction techniques described below, create a model no larger than 6 by 8 inches of a whimsical building. This building must be out of the ordinary. Perhaps it can be a house for a rock star, a restaurant for alligators, a library for bookworms. Emphasize the exterior appearance. Follow these steps:

Step 1. With a rolling pin or slab roller, roll out slabs of red or white clay ½ inch thick.

Step 2. Cut out cardboard templates for the parts of your building (roof, front, back, sides, base). Use a pencil or other pointed object to trace the outlines onto the clay.

Step 3. With a clay tool or blunt kitchen knife, cut the clay along the lines.

Step 4. To assemble the building, use the clay tool or blunt knife to mark Xs into the clay edges to be joined. Mix equal amounts of water and clay to make a *slip*. Paint the edges of the clay with the slip and carefully press them together. Start with the base and add the walls. Reinforce the interior with crumpled up paper. Leave the paper inside and add the roof.

Step 5. Put in or cut out windows, doors, and porches. Add architectural details by lightly carving them into the clay, or by attaching small pieces of clay using the score and slip method. Remember to make the design unusual.

Step 6. After the piece has dried thoroughly, paint on underglazes; fire it in a ceramics kiln. If you do not want to use underglazes for decoration, acrylic paints work well after the bisque (first) firing. Be creative and original. Be whimsical!

6-18: DESIGNING WITH NATURE:
SOURCES FOR ARCHITECTURAL DESIGNS

Create a nature motif for an architectural design. Pick one or two shapes from nature, such as a leaf, bean, honeycomb, shell, sand dollar, or flower. Draw or trace these objects. Repeat the shapes over and over again in a design that you will use in a building. You can create an overall design for a wall panel, ceiling, or door, or you can make a window surround or stained glass window. The shape will take on new meaning as a pattern, and the way in which you integrate shape, color, and texture will generate visual interest. Compare your design with those of others in your class.

6-19: DESIGNING WITH PATTERN IN ARCHITECTURE

Architects use patterns to create visual variety, interest, and a sense of uniqueness. Some patterns are very elaborate; others are simplistic, even plain. The sun's rays create patterns when they hit the surfaces of buildings.

Step 1. Select a type of building such as a high-rise apartment, vacation home, suburban home, new library, supermarket, or public swimming pool. Cut out a cardboard facade or outline of the building.

Step 2. Select one or two materials—toothpicks, Popsicle sticks, straws, wooden ice cream spoons, cotton swabs, wire, or balsa wood—to create a pattern in your facade. Be sure to put in doors and windows. Lay out the pattern and, when you are satisfied, glue the pieces down.

Step 3. Paint the finished facade, using only white or a light color.

Step 4. Turn the classroom lights off and use a spotlight or bright flashlight to illuminate the decorated facade. Examine the different effects created when light hits the various textures.

6-20: CREATING A MOOD WITH COLOR AND FORM

This is your opportunity to design a three-dimensional model of a pretty wild looking structure! Your major focus is to use color and form to create a feeling or mood for the building and its use. You might choose to design an aquarium, an amusement park, a special animal house at a zoo, a drive-in restaurant, a tennis or swim club, an arena for a sports team, a hotel for a theme part, a visitors' center for a special museum or concert hall, or anything else your imagination leads you to.

Step 1. Select the type of building you want to design. Sketch the building from various angles (front, back, sides, top).

Step 2. Select the colors that will set the mood for that type of building. Use watercolors to experiment with a series of colors, seeing how well the colors will work together.

Step 3. After you have decided on the final color scheme, create a three-dimensional model of your building to scale. Put the finished model on display and discuss with your classmates the mood they feel your colors create.

Step 4. Perhaps you can ask a professional architect to come to the class and critique the designs, reflecting on the purpose, colors, and moods of each building.

6-21: INTERIOR DESIGN: A MOOD COLLAGE USING ANALOGOUS COLORS

Color is an important component in the interior of a building. To see its effects, experiment with walls and furniture.

Step 1. Look up the word *analogous* in the dictionary and discuss what it means in relation to color.

Step 2. Each student selects one color. Be sure that you and your classmates choose the widest variety of colors possible.

Step 3. Find a wide variety of shades of the color you chose in magazines, paper scraps, and fabrics. For example, if your color is blue, look at a color wheel and notice that the range runs from purple-blue to blue to blue-green. You will find different intensities, too, from bright blue to dull blue.

Step 4. Cut your samples into 4-by-6-inch pieces and glue them to a piece of posterboard.

Step 5. Cut from magazines pictures of furniture and decorative objects used in buildings (sofas, chairs, tables, vases). Place them on the various colored backgrounds. How do the background colors affect the objects? Move them around until you find the combination you like the best. Continue the experiment by placing your furniture cut-outs on other students' color backgrounds.

Step 6. Make a chart that shows what happens visually to each object when it is placed on each background. Use a column for each color and a row for each object, forming a matrix. In each box, write a few descriptive words that express how the objects look on each background color.

Step 7. Go back to your original color board and glue your furniture to the backgrounds you prefer. Display these color-mood collages and study them for their visual impact.

Architecture Everywhere, © 2000 Zephyr Press, Tucson, Arizona

6-22: SKETCHING BUILDINGS ON LOCATION

Take a field trip to an interesting street with nice old buildings or a historic site in your city. What styles of architecture do you see? Select a building. Using drawing pencils and white drawing paper, capture the shapes and forms of at least three buildings on paper. The one- and two-point perspective skills you learned will come in handy here. Use cross-hatching, shading, or stippling drawing techniques to capture the details and architectural elements of the buildings. See samples in the appendix (page 203). Be sure to use dark, medium, and light values in your drawings.

6-23: STUDYING THE POSTMODERN DESIGN: CREATING WITH SYMMETRY

Using the example in the appendix (page 204) and classical or postmodern elements, sketch a facade. Include several window types, a door, and columns that could be copied and repeated to give the facade a sense of rhythm. Use only a black felt tip pen to add details. Include as many examples as possible.

6-24: MAKING THE BEST FANTASY CASTLE

Everyone is intrigued by old castles. You have probably seen examples in pictures, films, or video games. Maybe you have even visited a castle in another country. To get some starting ideas, look up some castles in books or on the Internet. From strips or pieces of balsa wood, scrap wood, cardboard, or found objects, construct an imaginary castle for some imaginary creature. Include the inhabitants who will live in the castle. The scale of the castle must be compatible with the creatures who live there: windows, doors, turrets, and other architectural features must be of a size the creature could actually use.

6-25: A MAKEOVER FOR YOUR CITY

If you could make over, redesign, or remodel your city, how would you do it?

Step 1. List all the things you would change, and why. Combine your list with those of others to make a class list. Discuss and agree on the changes most would want to make.

Step 2. Draw up a master plan that outlines the city. Keep the historically and architecturally significant buildings, and add others that would benefit and positively influence the appearance and design of the city while meeting the needs of the people who live and work there.

Step 3. Work with your architectural firm. Each group will have a 4-by-4-foot or 4-by-8-foot piece of plywood on which to build their model structure. You can use cardboard, mat board, foam board, or balsa wood for the buildings themselves. Build your models on a scale of 1 inch = 1 foot. Remember, each building affects the others. Experiment with the design of your building until the proportions are correct, and check with other groups to ensure that the buildings are proportional to one another and to the city overall.

Step 4. Lay out the buildings in a large space, such as the gym or playground. Add streets and landscaping. You can spray the model all one color or paint it in realistic colors. You might add small name markers to identify the buildings.

Step 5. Photograph your reconstructed town. You might invite the city council or city planners to see your work.

6-26: DESIGNING A PLACE FOR WORSHIP

For centuries, some of humans' most eloquent architectural accomplishments have been in houses of worship. This activity gives you the opportunity to create a three-dimensional model of a church, temple, mosque, or meeting house. The objective is to create a point of emphasis in your design.

Step 1. Study photographs of old and modern spiritual gathering places. Find at least five examples that are significantly different from each other. Notice the features that make them unique.

Step 2. Sketch a design for your building. Select one element in your structure that you will draw attention to or emphasize. It can be a color, shape, texture, or form.

Step 3. Use a cardboard box, scraps of posterboard or foam board, empty food containers, or other materials to create your building. Use scissors, mat cutters, or utility knives to cut the cardboard. Be sure to put a scrap of cardboard under the materials to protect the table or counter surface.

Step 4. Connect the edges of your forms with masking tape or hot glue. Paint the model with school acrylic paint or cover it with paper.

Step 5. In your imagination, become the point of emphasis. Write a poem that communicates how you, as this emphasis, move and inspire those who come to this house of worship.

Step 6. Display your house of worship with those of your classmates and read your poems. Compare the points of emphasis in each design and the manner in which these voices "speak."

Architecture Everywhere, © 2000 Zephyr Press, Tucson, Arizona

6-27: DEVELOPING THE CITY SKYLINE

Do you live in a large city? If not, have you ever visited one and noticed its skyline? Visit or find pictures of some of the most famous skylines in the United States: New York, San Francisco, Chicago, and others. What features are interesting and unique? What one area seems to be the visual emphasis of each city? What makes it stand out?

Use cardboard or posterboard to create a three-dimensional model of a city skyline. Cut the cardboard into the desired shapes and arrange them so the skyline stands on its own. Select one to be the visual emphasis of the city and build around it. Paint the city and display it in the classroom. See if you can identify the visual emphasis in each of your classmate's skylines.

6-28: I'VE GOT RHYTHM

Rhythm is an important element in architecture, as it is in music. This activity will help you see the relationship between musical and architectural rhythm.

Step 1. Play several kinds of music—classical, rock, jazz, rap, and hip hop. Listen for the main rhythms of each, the pattern that is repeated. As you listen, feel the movement. Note the picture or image that comes to mind, one that reflects the movement or rhythm of the music.

Step 2. For each kind of music, draw a shape or pattern that reflects how the rhythm feels to you.

Step 3. After you have completed a drawing for each kind of music, choose the drawing you like best. Repeat the shape or pattern over and over on a large piece of drawing paper. Use color as part of your rhythmic design.

Step 4. Make either a drawing or a model of a building. You might use one from a previous activity. Cut your drawn rhythm to fit your building; cover your building with the paper.

Step 5. Display your building along with those of your classmates, grouping those that represent each kind of musical rhythm. Compare the different types, and look for similarities within each group.

6-29: MY DREAM HOME:
FROM DESIGN TO FLOOR PLAN TO MODEL

You have explored the elements and principles of design that architects use to create beautiful and imaginative buildings. Think of them as ingredients you'll use in varying amounts to prepare a recipe for a tasteful and pleasing building. Using all your architectural skills and knowledge, apply the elements to design your dream home.

DESIGN

Step 1. Invite an architect to come talk to your class about how he or she begins to design a home. Your local office of the American Institute of Architects (AIA) will help you find one. You might even be able to visit the architect's office or a building site to see a dream house in progress.

Step 2. Look through popular magazines to get ideas for designs that appeal to you. Also, look at the professional magazines such as *Architectural Digest* and books on home design, which you can find in your local library or skim in a bookstore.

Step 3. Based on the information and ideas you gather, design your dream home. Draw the plans on graph paper, using a scale where $\frac{1}{4}$ inch = 1 foot. Prepare exterior views of the front, back, and sides. Draw the elevations of the house. Put in patios, decks, and the landscaping. Use colored pencils, watercolor markers, or watercolor paints to draw your plans on a good grade of drawing paper.

FLOOR PLAN

Step 1. Look again at the design magazines and books. Notice how the floor plans are drawn and how furniture is placed in the designs. Then look at some furniture pieces in magazines or stores and measure the length, width, and depth of some that appeal to you.

Step 2. Create a floor plan for one special room or even your entire dream house. Use graph paper or the worksheet in the appendix (page 198). Measure the room and record the measurements on paper. Calculate the measurements using the scale. Remember to include doors, windows, closets, offsets, and so on.

Step 3. Measure and cut out pieces of graph paper for each piece of furniture you are including in your design. Move the furniture around on the floor plan until you are pleased with the results. Then draw them in.

Step 4. Find some color and texture samples in magazines, material samples, wood scraps, vinyl flooring pieces, carpet, or wallpaper samples to show the color scheme you want for your special room.

MODEL

Step 1. In the same manner you have done in other projects, create a three-dimensional model of your dream house. Use foam board, cardboard, balsa wood, mat board, glue, markers, tape, and so on; be sure you keep to the correct scale (¼ inch = 1 foot).

Step 2. Apply an exterior finish to your house. You may want to use just the color of the materials or you may add color. Consider what surface pattern or texture you might want on the outside of your house. Use materials such as wood chips, cotton swabs, Popsicle sticks, or other materials to texture the exterior surface if you want. Paint your house or cover it with other coloring materials, such as paper.

Step 3. Mount your house on a base of plywood, vinyl tile, hardwood flooring, or cardboard. Add landscaping, decks, pools, or other outside areas.

Step 4. Display your model with those of your classmates. Take one another on a guided tour of your new construction, showing them the sketches, floor plans, and final model. Invite other classes, parents, or local architects to see your dream homes.

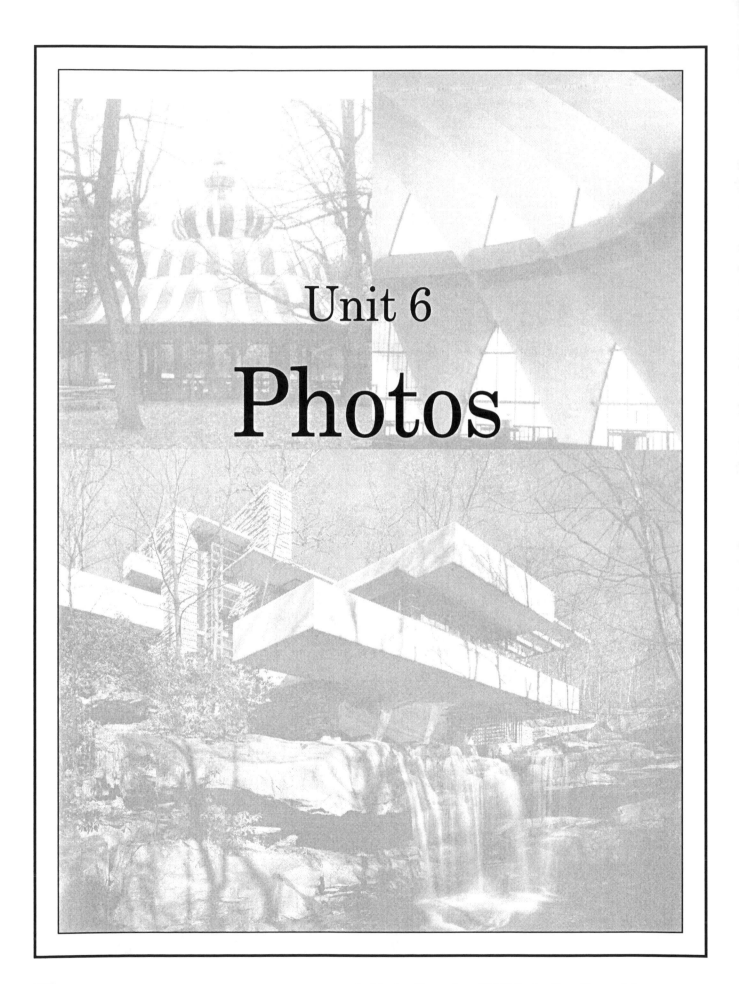

Unit 6
Photos

▲ FIGURE 6-1. THE ARCHITECT IS AT WORK HERE SURROUNDED BY DRAFTING TABLES AND BLUEPRINTS.

▲ FIGURE 6-2. THIS IS AN INTERIOR SKETCH OF A DESIGN FOR A NEW GYMNASIUM. (PHOTO COURTESY OF SOUTHERN ILLINOIS UNIVERSITY AT EDWARDSVILLE)

▲ FIGURE 6-3. THIS THREE-DIMENSIONAL MODEL IS OF A PROPOSED NEW ART AND DESIGN BUILDING FOR A UNIVERSITY. (PHOTO COURTESY OF SOUTHERN ILLINOIS UNIVERSITY AT EDWARDSVILLE)

▶ FIGURE 6-4. THE ARCHITECT'S DESIGNS ARE TRANSLATED INTO BLUEPRINTS.

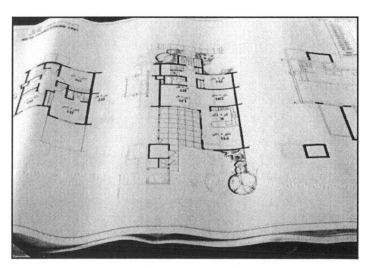

▲ FIGURE 6-5. THIS IS A MODEL OF FRANK O. GEHRY'S WALT DISNEY CONCERT HALL, TO BE BUILT IN LOS ANGELES, CALIFORNIA. (PHOTO COURTESY OF FRANK O. GEHRY & ASSOCIATES)

▲ FIGURE 6-6. HERE IS THE OHRSTOM LIBRARY AT ST. PAUL'S SCHOOL, CONCORD, NEW HAMPSHIRE, DESIGNED BY ROBERT A.M. STERN. HOW DOES HIS USE OF TRADITIONAL ARCHITECTURAL ELEMENTS FIT INTO THE EXISTING NEW ENGLAND ENVIRONMENT? (PHOTO COURTESY OF ROBERT A.M. STERN & ASSOCIATES)

     Architecture Everywhere, © 2000 Zephyr Press, Tucson, Arizona

▶ *FIGURE 6-7. IN THIS PHOTOGRAPH, FIND LINES IN NATURE. USE YOUR FINGER TO TRACE THE LINES.*

▶ *FIGURE 6-8. IMAGINE WALKING UP THIS SPIRAL STAIRCASE IN THE SHAKER FAMILY CENTRE TRUSTEES OFFICE, PLEASANT HILL, MERCER COUNTY, KENTUCKY. (PHOTO BY J-E. BOUCHER, COURTESY OF HABS)*

▶ *FIGURE 6-9. CIRCLES AND OVALS ARE USED IN THIS SKYLIGHT FOR A SHOPPING MALL.*

▶ *FIGURE 6-10. ORGANIC SHAPES ARE USED IN THE DESIGN OF THE MOTIF SEEN IN THIS CLOSE-UP OF A DECORATIVE PANEL.*

▲ *FIGURE 6-11. THIS PARK PAVILION (1871), IS FOUND IN TOWER GROVE PARK, ST. LOUIS, MISSOURI, AND IS LISTED ON THE NATIONAL REGISTER FOR HISTORIC PRESERVATION. ITS ROOF IS INSPIRED BY THE ONION OR BULB FORM.*

▲ *FIGURE 6-12. THE VAULTED ARCHES WERE MADE FROM POURED CONCRETE, WITH PIECES STACKED ON TOP OF EACH OTHER TO CREATE THE FORM USED IN THIS CHAPEL.*

▲ *FIGURE 6-13. SOME TEXTURAL MATERIALS USED IN ARCHITECTURE, SUCH AS GLASS, ARE SMOOTH AND REFLECT IMAGES.*

▶ *FIGURE 6-14. FIELD STONE HAS A ROUGH TEXTURE. IT HAS BEEN USED IN ARCHITECTURE FOR CENTURIES.*

▲ *FIGURE 6-15. A VISUAL PATTERN WAS CREATED IN THE FLOOR OF THE STATE OF ILLINOIS BUILDING IN CHICAGO, ILLINOIS. THE ARCHITECT HELMUT JAHN PURPOSE-FULLY USED REPEATED SHAPES, COLORS, AND TEXTURES TO CREATE A PATTERN THAT SERVES AS A FOCAL POINT FOR THIS MAGNIFICENT BUILDING, SEEN HERE FROM THE TOP FLOOR.*

▲ *FIGURE 6-16. REPEATED TRIANGLES IN THE INTERIOR OF THIS CHAPEL CREATE A SPIRAL, SHELL-LIKE PATTERN. THE EXTERIOR OF THE BUILDING APPEARS IN FIGURE 6-12.*

▲ *FIGURE 6-17. SYMMETRICAL BALANCE REFERS TO BUILDINGS THAT HAVE EQUAL OR SIMILAR ARCHITECTURAL ELEMENTS AND FEATURES ON EACH SIDE, AS SEEN IN THIS OLD JESUIT SEMINARY (1840–1849) IN FLORISSANT, MISSOURI.*

▲ *FIGURE 6-18. ASYMMETRICAL BALANCE IS USED IN A CONTEMPORARY OFFICE BUILDING.*

◀ *FIGURE 6-19. FRANK LLOYD WRIGHT'S 1937 MASTERPIECE, FALLINGWATER, WAS BUILT ON THE PRINCIPLE OF STACKED RECTANGULAR BLOCK FORMS BLENDING WITH THE NATURAL SURROUNDINGS. (HENDRICK BLESSING PHOTO, COURTESY OF THE CHICAGO HISTORICAL SOCIETY)*

◀ *FIGURE 6-20. THE CIRCULAR SHAPES AND TREE CREATE EMPHASIS.*

◀ *FIGURE 6-21. ARCH BRACKETS UNDER THE EAVES OF THIS BUILDING ALONG WITH DECORATIVE TERRA COTTA PANELS CREATE RHYTHM.*

Appendix

UNIT 1 MATERIALS

UNIT 5 MATERIALS

UNIT 6 MATERIALS

Family Group Information Inventory

Father _____

	Date	Place	Source
Birth			
Marriage			
Death			

Occupation _____

Military Service _____

Religious Affiliation _____

Other Marriages _____

Father _____

Mother _____

Mother _____

	Date	Place	Source
Birth			
Marriage			
Death			

Occupation _____

Religious Affiliation _____

Other Marriages _____

Father _____

Mother _____

Children (Start with Oldest)

Name	Birth (date)	Marriage (date)	Spouse's Name	Death (date)

FIVE-GENERATION FAMILY CHART

Research by _____

Address _____

_____

b = date of birth and place

m = date of marriage and place

d = date of death and place

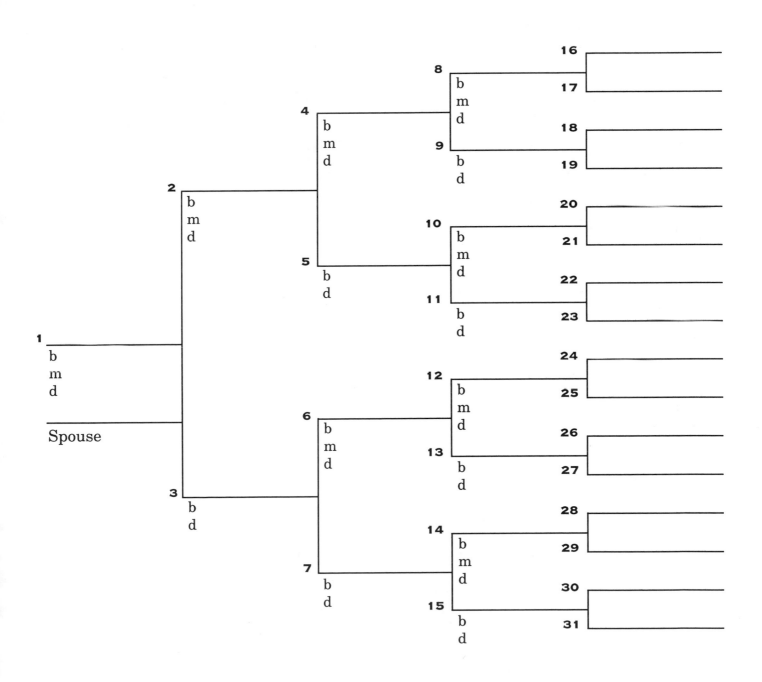

Design Your Room

You may use the items below to cut out, arrange, and then paste on the floor plan.
Use the black strips for the walls.

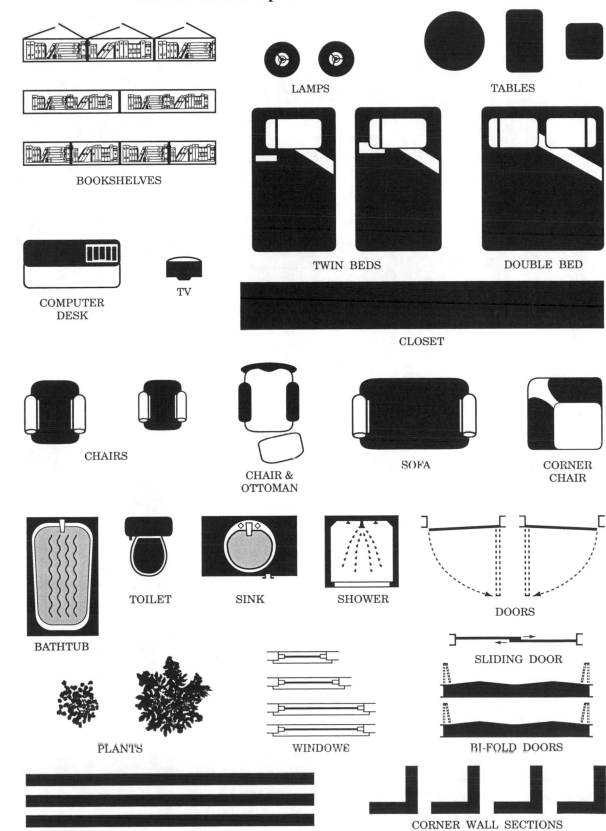

BOOKSHELVES

LAMPS

TABLES

COMPUTER
DESK

TV

TWIN BEDS

DOUBLE BED

CLOSET

CHAIRS

CHAIR &
OTTOMAN

SOFA

CORNER
CHAIR

BATHTUB

TOILET

SINK

SHOWER

DOORS

SLIDING DOOR

BI-FOLD DOORS

PLANTS

WINDOWS

CORNER WALL SECTIONS

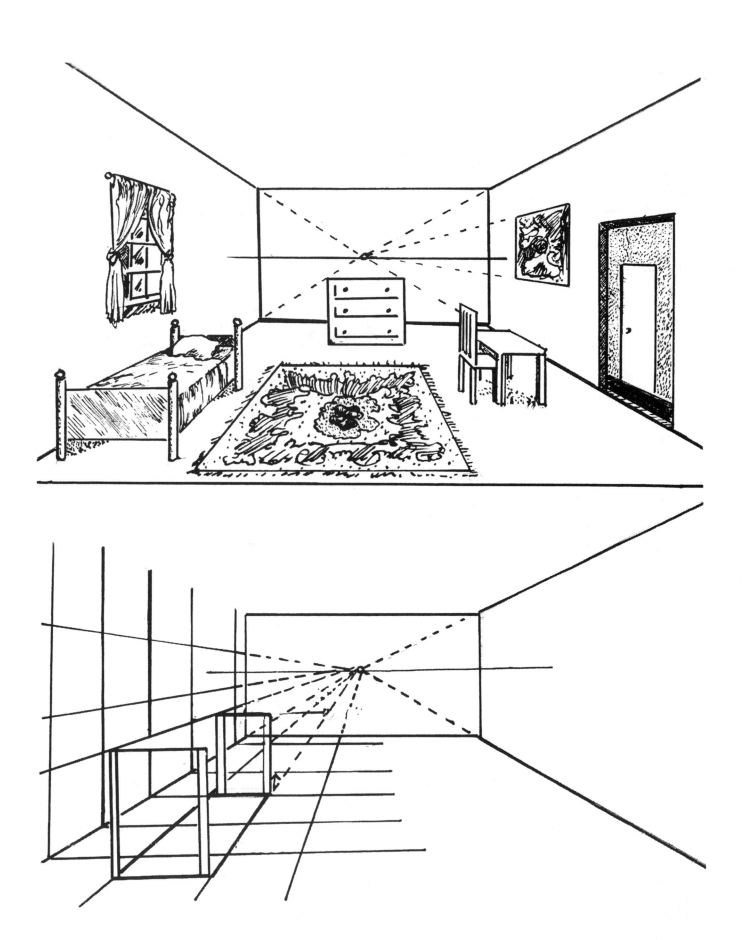

TWO-POINT PERSPECTIVE

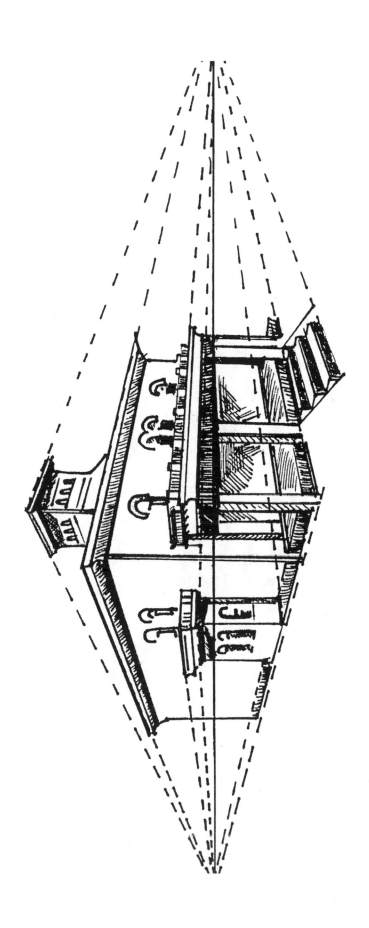

Figure 5-1. _y-shaped poles_
Figure 5-2. _notched-and-pegged beams_
Figure 5-3. _woven sticks and wattle and daub_
Figure 5-4. _thatch_
Figure 5-5. _chimney_
Figure 5-6. _applying clapboards_
Figure 5-7. _finished wall frame with window, door, and clapboards_
Figure 5-8. _felling trees_

1. _5 - 8_
2. _5 - 2_
3. _5 - 1_
4. _5 - 4_
5. _5 - 3_
6. _5 - 5_
7. _5 - 6_
8. _5 - 7_

UNIT 5 MATERIALS: THE EVOLUTION OF THE AMERICAN HOME
ANSWERS TO EXERCISES (PAGE 128)

_B_	Square notched
_C_	V-notched
_A_	Saddle notched
_E_	Full dovetail
_D_	Half dovetail

1. _5-9d_   _cutting down logs_
2. _5-9b_   _squaring the logs_
3. _5-9e_   _assembling the logs, rafters, roof_
4. _5-9a_   _constructing the chimney_
5. _5-9c_   _chinking between the logs_

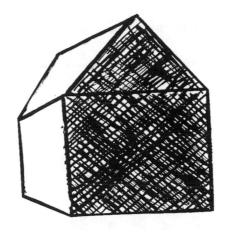

CROSS-HATCHING

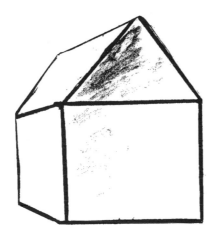

SHADING

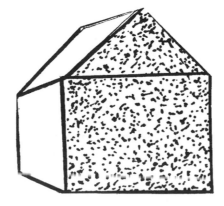

STIPPLING

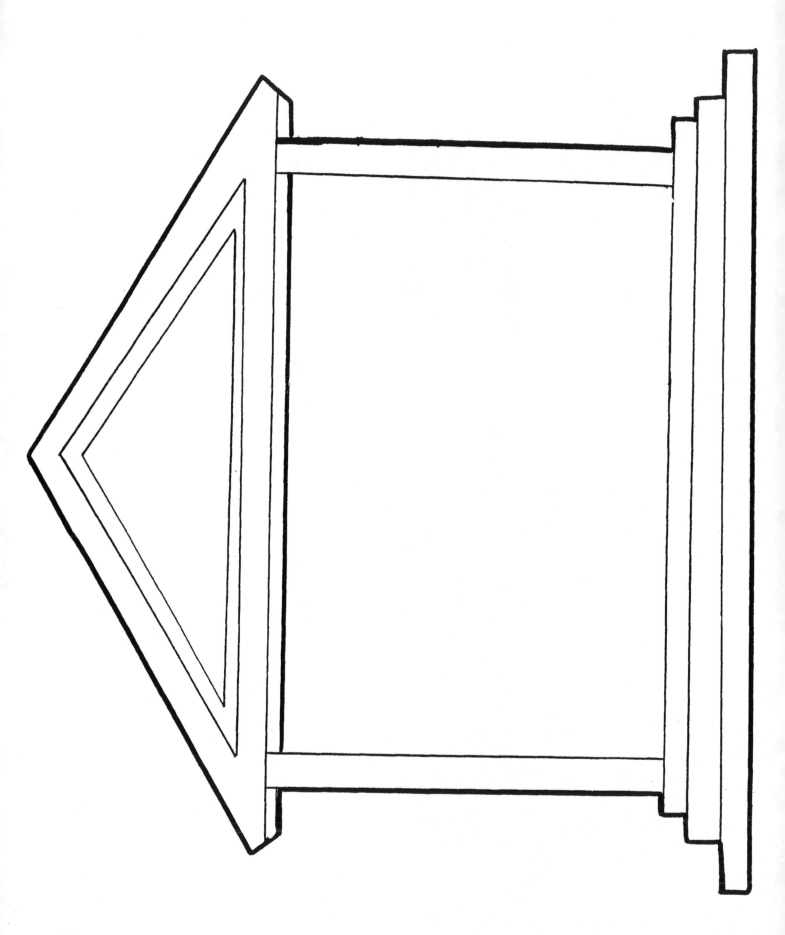

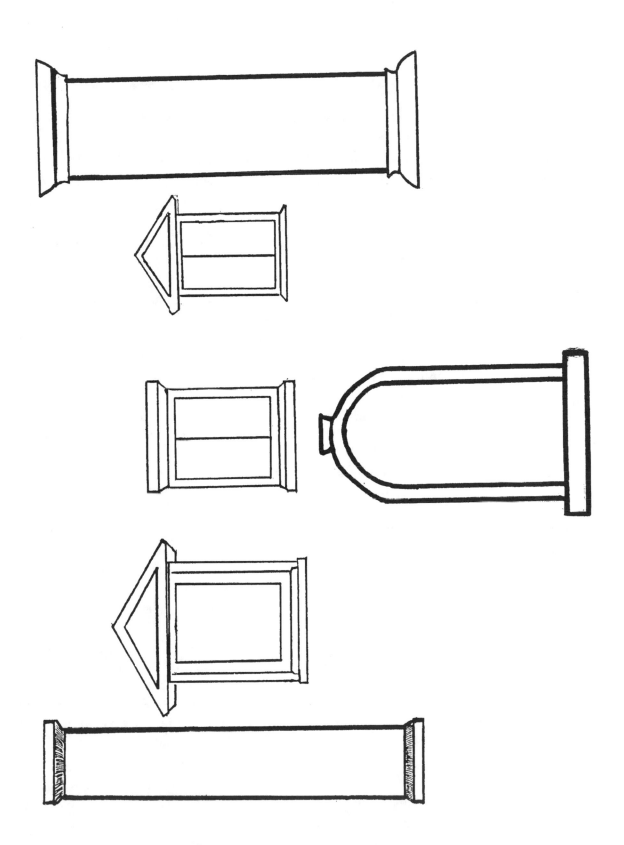

Glossary

arch: a method used to span an opening, usually rounded or pointed, often made from brick or stone.

architrave: the lowest division of an entablature that rests on the capital of a column.

asymmetry: balance that is not equal on each side of a dividing line (see symmetry).

balance: a principle of art; achieved either by the placement of objects in a symmetrical or an asymmetrical arrangement.

balloon framing: a nineteenth-century American method of wood frame construction built from small-dimensional sawn lumber, nailed together; all walls are weight-bearing with the upright studs running from sill to eaves.

baluster: an upright support of a handrail used in a staircase or as an upright, often decorative spindle used in a group to form a railing.

bargeboard: a decorative board covering the projecting rafter of the gable end of a roof, known also as a verge board; often found in Gothic revival architecture.

bas-relief: a type of sculpture in which the figures project only a little from the background.

batten: a narrow strip of wood used for flooring and often used on the vertical exterior siding of barns and outbuildings; board and batten refers to using battens to cover the seam where two pieces of vertical lumber meet. The batten creates a raised effect; when repeated, it creates its own pattern.

bay window: usually refers to a set of windows that are created by projecting these window units out of the exterior surface of the building; usually angular, curved, or bowed in appearance.

beam: a piece of lumber placed in a horizontal position supported on each end by a post.

belt course: refers to the use of brick or stone to create a horizontal band which projects from the surface of an exterior wall. Often separating two stones; often ornate and resembling a cornice.

bids: a term referring to estimates by a contractor for work on a specified project according to a plan.

bond: refers to the method of overlapping the mortar points of continuous courses of brick or stone, creating a wall; there are different types of bond; i.e., common, Flemish, English, etc.

bracket: a supporting piece of wood, stone, or other material to carry a projecting weight such as an eave, cornice, sill, or lintel; often found in Italianate style architecture.

canopy: a projection or hood over a door or window to provide shelter.

cantilever: a horizontal projection supported by a downward force behind a fulcrum; it is without external bracing and appears to be self-supporting; associated with the international and contemporary styles of architecture.

capital: the top or crowning feature of a column.

casement window: a type of window that opens outward on side hinges.

Architecture Everywhere, © 2000 Zephyr Press, Tucson, Arizona

clapboards: overlapping narrow horizontal boards, usually 4 to 6 inches wide, covering a wood-framed wall; sometimes called weatherboarding.

color: the characteristics of color are hue, value, and intensity; *hue* refers to the name of the color, *value* refers to the lightness or darkness or color going from black to white, and *intensity* refers to vividness, brightness, or dullness of a color; used in architecture to create interest and mood.

column: a supporting pillar, consisting of a base, shaft, and capital.

concrete: a building material consisting of cement mixed with coarse and fine pebbles, crushed stone, sand, and water in specific proportions.

corbel: a type of bracket found in some cornice work of brick buildings; formed by extending successive courses of brick so they stand out from the wall surface.

cornerstone: a cut stone or other material placed at the corner and base of a building with date of construction.

cornice: in classical architecture, the top projecting section of an entablature; also, any projecting ornamental moulding along the top of a building, wall, or window.

course: in a masonry wall, a single line or run of bricks or stone.

cresting: a decorative ridge or railing on a roof, usually of iron or wood.

cupola: a small square, circular, or polygonal-shaped structure situated at the top of the building, often with windows or vents; known also as a belvedere; seen in Greek revival and Italianate styles of architecture.

deconstructivism: an approach to architecture that questions the very nature of structures and buildings. Deconstructivists use unexpected structural forms, such as diagonals, jagged lines, trapezoids, and irregular, overlapping three-dimensional forms to challenge assumptions about what architectural form is and how it is defined. Deconstructivist architects working today include Frank O. Gehry and Peter Eisenman.

dentil: one of a series of small rectangular blocks or teeth applied as a decorative element in a cornice or belt course.

design: a preliminary sketch, plan, or outline; the arrangement of elements and principles of art.

dome: a vault of even curvature erected on a circular base; the shape can be semicircular, pointed, bulbous, or segmental.

dormer window: a window structure that projects from the slope of a roof.

double-hung window: a window consisting of two sashes placed side by side.

eave: the edge and underpart of a roof that projects over an outside wall.

elevation: a drawing made in projection in a vertical plane to show any one face or elevation of a building; the external views of a building.

emphasis: attempts at giving attention to something so it will stand out; a size, color, shape, or texture can be used.

entablature: in classical architecture, the portion of horizontal bands above the columns, consisting of the architrave, frieze, and cornice.

facade: the face or front of a building.

fanlight: a window, often semicircular, over a door with radiating glazing bars resembling a fan; often used in Georgian and Federal style buildings.

fascia board: a flat horizontal band, usually of wood, running under the roof; associated with the entablature in classical architecture.

fenestration: a term referring to the arrangement of windows in a building.

finial: a formal ornament at the top of a gable, canopy, fencepost, gate, rooftop, or doorway.

floor plan: a scale drawing of the layout of rooms, halls, and so on, of one or more floors of a building.

fluting: shallow, concave grooves running vertically on the shaft of a column, pilaster, or other surface.

form: an outline of a shape or figure that has length, width, and depth; also, to mold something.

frieze: an ornamental band in a building as on the upper part of a wall, constructed of wood, stone, brick, or plaster.

fulcrum: the support about which a lever turns.

gable: the vertical end of a building from the eaves to the ridge.

gambrel roof: a curb roof with a lower, steeper slope and an upper, flatter one.

gazebo: a small lookout tower or summerhouse with a view, usually in a park or garden.

grout: mortar used with brick, stone, or tile; consisting of quick lime and a portion of fine sand.

hip: associated with *hip roof,* the external angle formed by four sloping sides of a roof meeting at a top ridge.

jambs: the upright side of an opening, in a wall, window, arch, or doorway.

joist: a timber laid horizontally to support a floor or ceiling.

keystone: the central or middle stone of an arch or rib vault.

landing: the section of flooring at the top of the stairs.

light: a section of a window sometimes referred to as a pane of glass.

line: a series of connected points which appear to be continuous; having several properties such as thick, thin, straight, curved, angular, wavy, long, or short; contributes to the look of the building by accenting the structural elements.

lintel: the horizontal beam that forms the upper member of a window or door frame and supports part of the structure above it.

mansard roof: a type of roof with four sides; the sides of the roof slope or angle upward and join a flat surface; there are no gables in this design; associated with the Second Empire style.

mantle: the decorative surround found on the interior around the chimney; sometimes referred to as the horizontal piece over the chimney opening.

masonry: in construction, the use of stone, brick, or tile set in mortar.

mass: the three-dimensional volume which occupies real space; volume and weight are properties of mass.

molding: a type of decorative stripping projecting from a wall.

motif: a main theme or subject to be elaborated on or developed; a repeated figure in a design.

mullion: a vertical post or other upright dividing a window or other opening.

muntin: the slender wood or metal rails that separate panes of glass in a window.

Architecture Everywhere, © 2000 Zephyr Press, Tucson, Arizona

newel: the wooden posts placed at the top and bottom of a flight of steps.

oculus: a round window.

offset: a horizontal ledge on the face of a wall.

order: in classical architecture a column with base, shaft, capital, and entablature; Doric, Tuscan, Ionic, and Corinthian are the major orders used in architecture.

ornament: any detail added to a building for decoration.

palladian window: an archway or window with three openings, the central one arched and wider than the others; usually rounded, named after Italian architect Palladio (1566–1750).

pattern: a repetition of shape, color, texture, line, or form organized into the overall design of a building.

pediment: the triangular space forming a roof or porch gable, also used in windows or doorways.

pilaster: an upright, flat, rectangular pillar projecting slightly from a wall.

pinnacle: a pointed ornament found at the top of a tower or roof.

pitch: the incline or rise of a roof.

porch: the covered entrance to a building; sometimes called a portico if columned and pedimented like a temple front.

porte cochere: the roof and its supporting structure extending from the entrance of a building over a driveway to shelter people getting in and out of vehicles.

postmodern architecture: architecture, primarily beginning in the late 1960s, that reacts in various ways to the purity and autonomy of such Modernist architecture as the International style; while postmodern architects employ Modern techniques, they often combine them with historical and/or vernacular architectural references, in order to create buildings and spaces that communicate with people and make visible links to community. Postmodern structures often employ familiar, traditional architectural symbolism (columns, gables, pediments, chimneys) in witty, ironic, and engaging ways; notably used by the architectural team of Robert Venturi and Denise Scott-Brown.

preservation: stabilizing and restoring a structure in its existing form by preventing further change or deterioration.

proportion: the relationships of parts to a whole; also, the relationship among the parts of a whole to each other: the concern about the relationships among size, space, volume, materials, and site of the building.

quoins: the dressed stones at the corners of buildings, usually laid so that their faces are alternately large and small; from the French word "coin," meaning corner; also can be seen in brick.

rafter: a support for the roof.

reconstruction: re-creation of a building from historical, archaeological, and architectural documents.

renovation: making selective use of any changes in structures and detail, leaving those features which may make the building more adaptable to modern use or to the people who will live in them; for example, individuals with disabilities.

restoration: rebuilding a structure to some specific historical time period or style, based on a given architectural design.

rhythm: the repetition of an artistic element or several elements to create visual harmony.

roof type: a type of roof that is designed based on given plans; examples include gable, shed, hip, mansard, gambrel, flat, conical, saltbox, and bellcast hip.

setback: distance a building is located from the property line or sidewalk.

shake: split wood shingle.

shape: v. to arrange, fashion, or express a plan; n. items that have length and width.

shed roof: a lean-to roof that has only one sloping surface.

siding material: such as wood boards, shingles, or metal used for surfacing a building.

sill: the exterior horizontal member on which a window frame rests.

slope: incline of roof expressed in inches of rise per foot of run.

soffit: the underside of the fascia board.

stained glass: pieces of colored glass held together by lead or other material used to create windows.

stucco: plaster for outside walls.

style: specific or characteristic manner of expression or a design; for example, Greek revival.

symmetry: balanced exactly the same on both sides of a center; an arrangement of features in both halves of an object or building that are equal (see *asymmetry*).

terra cotta: fired and glazed clay created from moulds; used mainly for wall coverings or ornamentation.

texture: the tactile property of a material's surface or the visual quality of how a texture would feel by looking at it.

transom: an opening over a door or larger window, often used for ventilation.

turret: a small, usually rounded slender tower.

unity: a oneness is achieved when all parts of a whole are satisfactorily combined to seem aesthetically pleasing.

vault: an arched ceiling or roof of stone, brick, or cement.

veranda: a long, open porch or balcony covered by a roof.

vernacular: the architecture of common people, often associated with a local region.

vestibule: an entry hallway, lobby, or porch.

waiscot: lower three or four feet on an exterior wall, when lined with paneling or other material differing from the rest of the wall.

window sash: a frame in which the panes of glass are set.

wing: an extension of a building with its length parallel to the length of the building.

Architecture Everywhere, © 2000 Zephyr Press, Tucson, Arizona

Bibliography for Teachers

Adler, Jerry. 1990. "The House of the Future." *Newsweek* Special Issue: 72.

Benton, William. 1973. *The Britannica Encyclopedia of American Art.* New York: Simon and Schuster.

Bicknell, A. J. 1887. *Bicknell's Victorian Buildings.* New York: Dover.

Burroughs, Lea. 1988. *Introducing Children to the Arts: A Practical Guide for Librarians and Editors.* Boston: G. K. Hall.

Calloway, Stephen, and Elisabeth Cromley. 1991. *Elements of Style.* New York: Simon and Schuster.

Clark, Clifford Edward, Jr. 1986. *The American Family Home.* Chapel Hill, N.C.: North Carolina Press.

da Costa, Beverly, ed. 1971. *An American Heritage Guide: Historic Homes of America.* New York: American Heritage.

Fairbanks, J. 1975. *Frontier America.* Greenwich, Conn.: New York Graphic Society.

Fleming, J., H. Honour, and W. Pevsneer. 1986. *Dictionary of Architecture.* Middlesex, England: Penguin.

Gamburg, R., W. Kwak, M. Hutchings, and J. Altheim. 1988. *Learning and Loving It.* Portsmouth, N.H.: Heinemann Educational.

Hanser, D. A., and C. E. Morgan. 1984. *Uticitas, Firmitas, Venustas: Architecture and Society.* Dubuque, Ia.: Kendall/Hunt.

Holden, C., G. Olsen, and M. Olsen. 1980. *Historic Preservation Education.* Champaign, Ill.: Educational Concepts.

Jett, S. C. 1981. *Navajo Architecture: Forms, History, Distributions.* Tucson, Ariz.: University of Arizona Press.

Jodidio, Philip. 1993. *Contemporary American Architects.* Koln, Germany: Taschen.

Laase, Lois, and Joan Clemmons. 1998. *The Best Research Reports Ever.* New York: Scholastic.

McAlester, Virginia, and Lee McAlester. 1985. *A Field Guide to American Houses.* New York: Alfred A. Knopf.

Noble, Allen G. 1984a. *Houses. Wood, Brick, and Stone: The North American Settlement Landscape,* vol. 1. Amherst, Mass.: University of Massachusetts Press.

————. 1984b. *Barns and Farm Structures. Wood, Brick and Stone: The North American Settlement Landscape,* vol. 2. Amherst, Mass.: University of Massachusetts Press.

Olsen, G., and M. Olsen. 1980. *Archi-Teacher: A Guide to Architecture in the Schools.* Champaign, Ill.: Educational Concepts.

Pfeiffer, Bruce Books. 1991. *Frank Llyod Wright Selected Homes.* Tokyo, Japan: ADA Editor.

Reid, Richard. 1980. *A Book of Building: A Traveler's Guide.* London: Michael Joseph.

Rense, Paigne, ed. 1990. "The AD 100 Architects." *Architectural Digest* (August): 16–296.

Rifkind, Carole. 1980. *A Field Guide to American Architecture.* New York: Plume.

Schoel, Alan H. 1992. *United States History and Art.* Lake Forest, Ill.: Glencoe.

Shaefer, John. 1988. *Polariod Educational Program: Lesson Activity Book.* Cambridge, Mass.: Polaroid Corporation.

Thomsen, Kathleen Thorne. 1994. *Frank Lloyd Wright for Kids.* Chicago, Ill.: Chicago Review Press.

Ulack, John Michael. 1978. *The Afro American Tradition in Decorative Arts.* Cleveland, Ohio: Cleveland Museum of Art.

Walker, Lester. 1997. *American Shelter.* Woodstock, N.Y.: Overlook Press.

Whiffen, Marcus, and Frederick Koeper. 1987a. *American Architecture 1607–1860.* Cambridge, Mass.: MIT Press.

————. 1987b. *American Architecture 1860–1976.* Cambridge, Mass.: MIT Press.

Wood, Ernst. 1992. *Historic Homes of America.* New York: Smithmark.

Bibliography for Students

Adams, Simon. 1991. *Explore the World of Manmade Wonders*. Racine, Wis.: Western.

Alessi, Jean, and Jane Miller. 1987. *Once upon a Memory: Your Family Tales and Treasures*. White Hall, Va.: Betterway.

Allen, Judy, Earldene McNeill, and Velma Schmidt. 1992. *Cultural Awareness for Children*. Menlo Park, Calif.: Addison-Wesley.

Anno, Mitsumasa. 1983a. *Anno's Country House*. New York: Philomel.

———. 1983b. *Anno's U.S.A.* New York: Philomel.

Architecture and Construction. 1994. New York: Scholastics.

Bare, Colleen Stanley. 1992. *This Is a House*. New York: Dutton Cobblchill.

Barnard, Bob. 1993. *A Time to Harvest: The Farm Painting of Franklin Halverson*. Mount Horeb, Wis.: Midwest Traditions.

Beard, D. C. 1972. *Shelters, Shacks, and Shanties*. New York: Charles Scribner.

Beeler, Susan Provost. 1989. *Roots for Kids: A Genealogy Guide for Young People*. White Hall, Va.: Betterway.

Borg, Mary. 1989. *Writing Your Life*. Fort Collins, Colo.: Cottonwood Press.

Cole, Alison. 1992. *Perspective*. London: Dorling Kindersley.

Croom, Emily Ann. 1989. *Unpuzzling Your Past: A Basic Guide for Young People*. White Hall, Va.: Betterway.

D'Alelio, Jane. 1989. *I Know That Building*. Washington, D.C.: Preservation Press.

Dupré, Judith. 1996. *Skyscrapers*. New York: Black Dog, Leventhal.

Gaughenbaugh, Michael, and Herbert Camburn. 1993. *Old House, New Home*. Washington, D. C.: Preservation Press.

Gintzler, A. S. 1994. *Rough and Ready Homesteaders*. Santa Fe, N.M.: John Muir.

Glenn, Patricia Brown. 1993. *Under Every Roof*. Washington, D.C.: Preservation Press.

Green, Fayall. 1991. *The Anatomy of a House*. New York: Doubleday.

Greenwood, Barbara. 1994. *A Pioneer Sampler*. Boston: Houghton Mifflin.

Gulliford, Andrew. 1991. *America's Country Schools.* Washington, D.C.: Preservation Press.

Haas, Irvin. *Houses of American Authors.* Washington, D.C.: Preservation Press.

Hechtlinger, Adelaide. 1986. *The Seasonal Hearth: The Woman at Home in Early America.* Woodstock, N.Y.: Overlook Press.

Hughes, Langston. 1995. *The Block.* New York: Metropolitan Museum of Art.

Isaacson, Philip M. 1988. *Round Buildings, Square Buildings, and Buildings That Wiggle like a Fish.* New York: Alfred A. Knopf.

Ketchum, William C. 1996. *Grandma Moses.* New York: Smithmark.

Klein, Marilyn W., and David P. Fogle. 1985. *Clues to American Architecture.* Washington, D.C.: Starhill Press.

Lewis, R. K. 1987. *Master Builders: A Guide to Famous American Architects.* Washington, D.C.: Preservation Press.

Longstreth, Richard. 1987. *The Building of Main Street: A Guide to American Commerical Architecture.* Washington, D.C.: Preservation Press.

Macaulay, David. 1980. *Unbuilding.* Boston: Houghton Mifflin.

MacDonald, Fiona. 1994. *Timeless Houses, Habitats, and Home Life.* New York: Franklin Watts.

Maddox, Diane, ed. 1985. *Built in the U.S.A.* Washington, D.C.: Preservation Press.

Naylor, David. 1987. *Great American Movie Theaters.* Washington, D.C.: Preservation Press.

Norwich, John. 1988. *The World Atlas of Architecture.* New York: Portland House.

Phillips, Allen. 1993. *Who Built That Secaucus?* Englewood Cliffs, N.J.: Chartwell Books.

Phillip, Steven. 1992. *Old House Dictionary.* Washington, D.C.: Preservation Press.

Poppeliers, John Chambers, Jr., S. Allen, and Nancy B. Schwartz. 1984. *What Style Is It? A Guide to American Architecture.* Washington, D.C.: Preservation Press.

Provenzo, E., Jr., A. B. Provenzo. 1984a. *Oral History Photographs, Family History, Cemeteries.* Menlo Park, Calif.: Addison Wesley.

———. 1984b. *Map and Mapping, City and Neighborhood Architecture.* Menlo Park, Calif.: Addison Wesley.

Simmons, Lee, ed. 1996. *Family History: A DK First Activity Pack*. London: Dorling Kindersley.

Smith, Mary Lou M. 1998. *Grandmother's Adobe Dollhouse*. Albuquerque, N.M.: Route 66.

Tishler, William. 1989. *American Landscape Architecture: Designers and Places*. Washington, D.C.: Preservation Press.

Van der Meer, Ron, and Deyan Fudjic. 1997. *The Architecture Pack*. New York: Alfred A. Knopf.

Van Tscharner, Renata, and Ronald Lee Fleming. 1993. *Changing American Cityscapes*. Palo Alto, Calif.: Dale Seymour.

Wilder, Laura Ingalls. 1932. *Little House in the Big Woods*. New York: HarperCollins.

————. 1935. *Little House on the Prairie*. New York: HarperCollins.

Wilkerson, Philip. 1995. *Building*. New York: Alfred A. Knopf.

Winters, Nathan B. 1986. *Architecture Is Elementary*. Salt Lake City, Utah: Gibbs M. Smith.

Unit 5, Architectural Adventure 5-10

Brink, Carol Ryrie. 1999. *Caddie Woodlawn*. New York: Simon and Schuster.

Dragonwagon, Crescent. 1990. *Home Place*. New York: MacMillan.

Haugaard, Kay. 1999. *No Place*. Minneapolis, Minn.: Milkweed Editions.

Patterson, Katherine. 1977. *Bridge to Terabithia*. New York: HarperCollins.

Pryor, Bonnie. 1987. *The House on Maple Street*. New York: W. Morrow.

Shelby, Anne. 1995. *Homeplace*. New York: Orchard.

Taylor, Mildred D. 1976. *Roll of Thunder, Hear My Cry*. New York: Dial Press.

Wilder, Laura Ingalls. 1932. *Little House in the Big Woods*. New York: HarperCollins.

————. 1935. *Little House on the Prairie*. New York: HarperCollins.

Teach Math and Science Standards with a Fun New Twist!

MAKING MAGNIFICENT MACHINES
Fun with Math, Science, and Engineering
by Carol McBride
Grades K–8

Guide your students through practical construction applications with projects they assemble from recycled materials. Science as inquiry becomes part of building the machines. Choose from fourteen step-by-step projects that emphasize key concepts of—

- Potential, kinetic, and electrical energy
- Inclined plane
- Fulcrum, lever, and pulley and more!

1104-W . . . $22

SING A SONG OF SCIENCE
by Kathleen Carroll, M.Ed.
Grades K–6

featuring Gwendolyn Jenifer and the students of the Duke Ellington School of the Arts

You'll find indispensable tools to reinforce science concepts you're already teaching. Explore these new dimensions in learning—

- Stories—the George Washington Carver story
- Raps—tropical rain forest rap, energy rap
- Songs—matter song, classifying song
- Resources—brain-based teaching overview, annotated references, web connections, and musical scores

35-minute audiotape and 64-page activity manual
1094-W . . . $27

Order Form ☎ Please include your phone number in case we have questions about your order.

Qty.	Item #	Title	Unit Price	Total
	1104-W	Making Magnificent Machines	$22	
	1094-W	Sing a Song of Science	$27	

Name _____

Address _____

City _____

State _____ Zip _____

Phone (_____) _____

E-mail _____

Method of payment (check one):
- ❑ Check or Money Order   ❑ Visa
- ❑ MasterCard   ❑ Purchase Order Attached

Credit Card No. _____

Expires _____

Signature _____

Subtotal	
Sales Tax (AZ residents, 5%)	
S & H (10% of subtotal–min $4.00)	
Total (U.S. funds only)	

CANADA: add 22% for S & H and G.S.T.

100% SATISFACTION GUARANTEE
If at any time, for any reason, you're not completely satisfied with your purchase, return your order in saleable condition for a 100% refund (excluding shipping and handling). No questions asked!

Call, Write, or FAX for your FREE Catalog!

Zephyr Press ®
REACHING THEIR HIGHEST POTENTIAL

P.O. Box 66006-W
Tucson, AZ 85728-6006

1-800-232-2187
520-322-5090
FAX 520-323-9402

Order these resources and more any time, day or night, online at http://zephyrpress.com